GO ▶ scuba dive

Monty Halls

London, New York, Melbourne, Munich, and Delhi

This book is dedicated to **Mark Rogers**—a Royal Marine, an outstanding diver, and a man who chose to live life to the full. Sleep well buddy.

Editor **Bob Bridle**
Project Editor **Richard Gilbert**
Senior Art Editor **Susan St. Louis**
Design by **On Fire**
Production Editor **Sarah Sherlock**
Production Controller **Inderjit Bhullar**
Managing Editor **Stephanie Farrow**
Managing Art Editor **Lee Griffiths**
Photography **Matt Oldfield**

DVD produced for Dorling Kindersley by
Scubazoo www.scubazoo.com
Director/Camera **Roger Munns**
Director/Narrator **Monty Halls**
Editor **Jonni Isaacs**
Online Editor **KB.Lai**
Music by **Brollyman**

First American Edition, 2007

Published in the United States by
DK Publishing
375 Hudson Street
New York, New York 10014

07 08 09 10 11   10 9 8 7 6 5 4 3 2 1

A catalog record for this book is available from the Library of Congress.

ISBN: 978-0-75662-627-3

DK books are available at special discounts when purchased in bulk for sales promotions, premiums, fund-raising, or educational use. For details, contact: DK Publishing Special Markets, 375 Hudson Street, New York, New York 10014 or SpecialSales@dk.com. Color reproduction by Wyndeham Pre-Press, UK. Printed and bound in China by Hung Hing.

Discover more at
www.dk.com

contents

how to use this book and DVD

This fully integrated book and accompanying DVD are designed to inspire you to get in the water and start diving. Watch all the essential techniques on the DVD in crystal-clear, real-time footage, with key elements broken down in state-of-the-art digital graphics, and then read all about them, and more, in the book.

Using the book

Descending underwater for the first time can seem a daunting prospect, so this book explains everything you need to know to go diving with safety and confidence. Cross-references to the DVD are included on pages that are backed up by footage.

Switch on the DVD

When you see this logo in the book, check out the action in the relevant chapter of the DVD.

Using the DVD

Supporting the book with movie sequences and computer graphics, the DVD is the perfect way to see key techniques demonstrated in precise detail. Navigate to each subject using the main menu, and view sequences as often as you like to see how it's done!

Flick to the book

When you see this logo on the DVD, flick to the relevant page of the book to read all about it.

why scuba dive?

Modern-day diving is far removed from the mysterious environment of yesteryear. Gone is the impression that a man-eating monster lurks around every corner, or that divers must be superhuman athletes. Through advances in equipment and technology, the sport is now accessible to virtually everyone, regardless of age or fitness. These developments, together with a growing fascination for the marine environment, mean scuba diving has never been so popular.

The secret to good diving is in the title of this book—go scuba dive. There is simply no substitute for experience. By happy coincidence, the recreational diving industry has never been in better shape, so there really is nothing to stop you. Diving does demand a certain level of training (it's still regarded as an extreme sport), and this book should act as a useful tool as you develop your skills. Once you have achieved your first open-water qualification, I also hope it inspires you to explore the wonders of the underwater world.

go for it!

coming up...

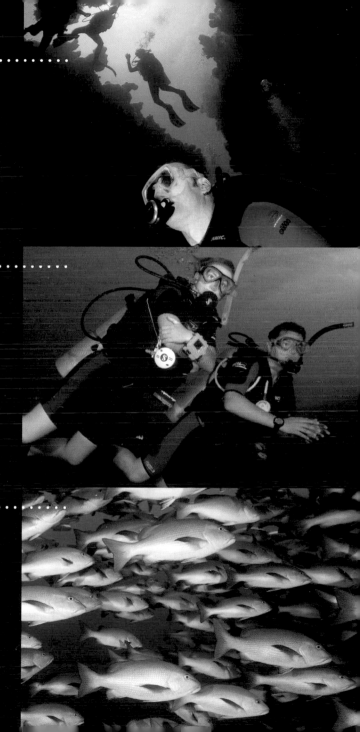

The goal: 18–21

For many new divers, their first experience of being underwater is one of the most rewarding of their diving careers. Find out what's in store when you descend beneath the surface.

Diving classifications: 22–25

The principle of any form of diving is to support life beneath the water's surface in order to explore the underwater world. There are, however, specializations to suit every taste and interest. Diving techniques cover all aspects of the sport, from casual resort diving to extreme technical exploration.

The marine realm: 26–29

The main reason to go scuba diving is to immerse yourself in the underwater realm. The ocean fringes of the world are rich with an array of marine life and ecosystems that vary with latitude and location. These waters offer a range of fascinating diving experiences.

an underwater odyssey

The mountains that skirt the shore seem to offer little in terms of life, shimmering in the heat, stark and barren in the relentless glare of the sun. It is only when I glance down that a hint of what is to come reveals itself, dark shapes twisting and flashing beneath the stern platform of the dive vessel, moored in a wide sweep of bay.

Making a final adjustment to my gear, I exchange a swift, final OK with my buddy, his eyes wrinkled in a smile behind his mask, before I turn and step into another world.

After the initial disorientation of breaking the surface, it takes a moment for me to right myself, and for the mist of bubbles and foam created by my entry to clear. Peering into the sapphire middle-distance, I can see the reef wall, plunging into the darkness on the edge of the continental shelf. Finning down toward it, it seems to come to life as I get closer, pulsing, swaying, and twitching with a million tiny forms.

continued >

an underwater odyssey (continued)

The waters play host to thousands of fish species, swirling over a multicolored array of corals and sponges. Arriving at the reef wall, I hover a short distance away, feeling like some flying visitor to a mountainous rainforest, with shoals of kaleidoscopic, neon antheas and damselfish moving in unison over massive coral heads before me.

Glancing at my buddy, I see him gesture toward a deep cut in the reef wall. Gently exhaling, I drop toward it, slipping through the entrance into the very heart of the reef itself. Countless generations of coral have created a twisting tunnel, illuminated only by the eerie blue of the sun pouring through the entrance. We fly through the canyon, turning along stark walls and under dark overhangs, before emerging once again to soar out into the blue of open water, the reef wall fading away behind us.

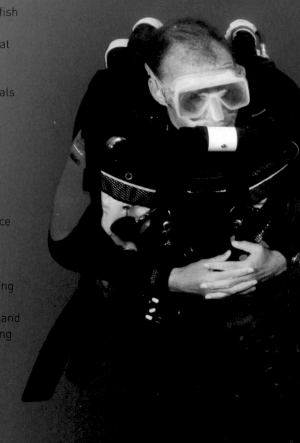

forms of diving

continued >

Recreational diving, as opposed to commercial or professional diving, is the most popular form of the sport. It is enjoyed by people of all ages for the pure joy of exploring the underwater world. There are, however, many other forms of diving, including everything from advanced technical diving at depth, to snorkeling in the shallows. All diving disciplines share the common principle of sustaining human life underwater.

a

The development of diving

Diving as we know it today first appeared with the development of the aqualung, during World War II. However, people have long had the urge to explore beneath the waves, whether in search of food and riches, or out of sheer curiosity.

Archeological research shows that free divers were collecting oysters from the seabed as far back as 3,000 BCE. In the 4th century BCE, Aristotle records the first use of a diving bell, made from an upturned cauldron filled with air. By around 1500, Leonardo da Vinci had designed equipment for underwater exploration, including snorkels and bags that could deliver air to a diver. The breakthrough in diving technology came in 1943, when Jacques Cousteau and Emile Gagnan designed and tested the regulator and aqualung, heralding the modern scuba age.

a Snorkeling
A form of diving in its own right, snorkeling simply involves breathing through a J-shaped tube while swimming near the surface of the water.

b Recreational diving
The majority of divers practice the sport as a hobby, often while on vacation in tropical locations. Recreational diving usually involves breathing compressed air and staying within conservative depth and decompression limits.

b

WATCH IT
see DVD chapter 1

forms of diving (continued)

Technical diving

This form of diving is at the cutting edge of dive technology and adventure. Developed by divers exploring deep into caves and inaccessible wrecks, mixed-gas diving involves the use of complex gas mixtures and multiple cylinders that allow divers to go deeper and stay under for longer. Rebreather diving, using gear that recycles exhaled air, is another popular form of technical diving. Both require special training and meticulous planning.

Free diving

There are a number of disciplines in free diving, but the concept is always to remain immersed for as long as possible on a single breath. We are all free divers to a certain extent, with anyone who has ever held their breath and ducked beneath the surface being a free diver. However, the extreme forms of the sport are the preserve of truly extraordinary athletes.

C

d

WATCH IT
see DVD chapter 1

the oceans and marine life

Around 70 percent of Planet Earth's surface is covered in water, so a more appropriate name might be Planet Ocean.

Much of this water is inaccessible to the recreational diver, with the average depth of the world's oceans an incredible 2½ miles (4 km). However, most marine life clusters around the shallow coastal fringes, known as the continental shelf, where sunlight filters through the water column, creating an abundance of tiny plants called phytoplankton—the basis of the marine food chain. The oceans can be split into three main regions.

a Tropical oceans
Home to the coral reef—the most vibrant and colorful of all marine ecosystems—the water temperature in the tropics generally remains above 68°F (20°C).

b Temperate oceans
These waters lie between the tropics and the poles. The changeable conditions here are perfect for a rich diversity of ecosystems, such as vast underwater forests of kelp.

c Polar waters
For the intrepid diver, the Arctic and Antarctic regions offer many attractions, such as the beluga whale. The water here is around 40°F (5°C) and below.

a

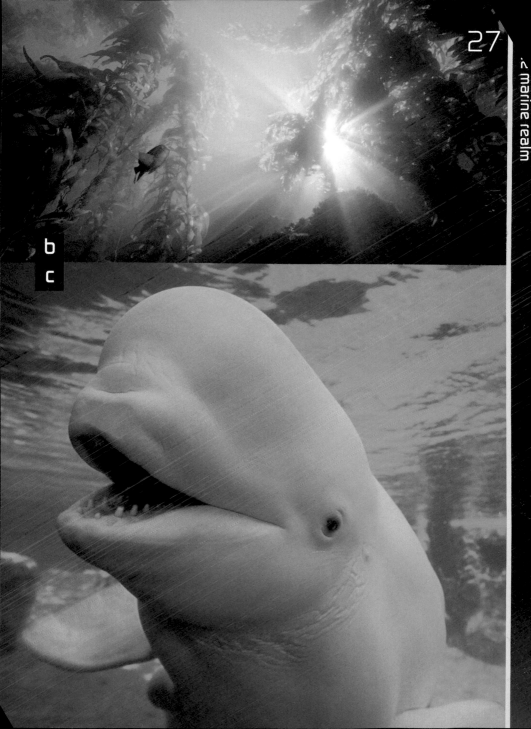

b
c

depth and pressure

Unlike marine mammals, with millions of years of evolution on their side, human beings must rely on technology and learned techniques to compensate for the effects of pressure underwater.

Aside from maintaining respiration and body temperature below the surface, coping with increased pressure at depth is the diver's most important consideration. The human body has three air spaces that feel the effects of a change in pressure—the inner ear, the sinuses, and the lungs. In line with Boyles Law (which states that the volume of a gas is inversely proportional to the pressure exerted on it), these air spaces attempt to decrease in size as pressure increases. To maintain volume in these spaces, the diver must introduce air.

How water affects light and sound
Your eyes can't focus underwater, so a mask, which places a pocket of air in front of them, is essential for any dive. Light travels more slowly in water than in air and bends (refracts) when it reaches your mask. As a result, objects appear closer and larger than they really are. Sound travels four times faster through water than air, making it difficult to ascertain the direction of a sound.

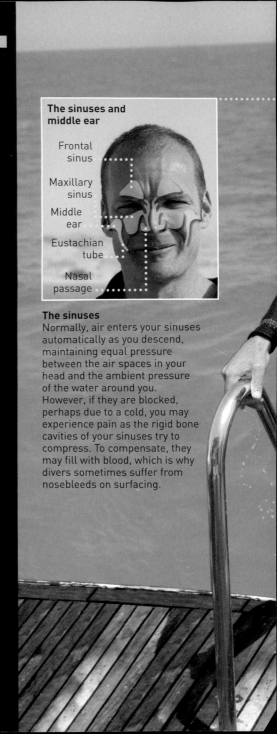

The sinuses and middle ear

Frontal sinus

Maxillary sinus

Middle ear

Eustachian tube

Nasal passage

The sinuses
Normally, air enters your sinuses automatically as you descend, maintaining equal pressure between the air spaces in your head and the ambient pressure of the water around you. However, if they are blocked, perhaps due to a cold, you may experience pain as the rigid bone cavities of your sinuses try to compress. To compensate, they may fill with blood, which is why divers sometimes suffer from nosebleeds on surfacing.

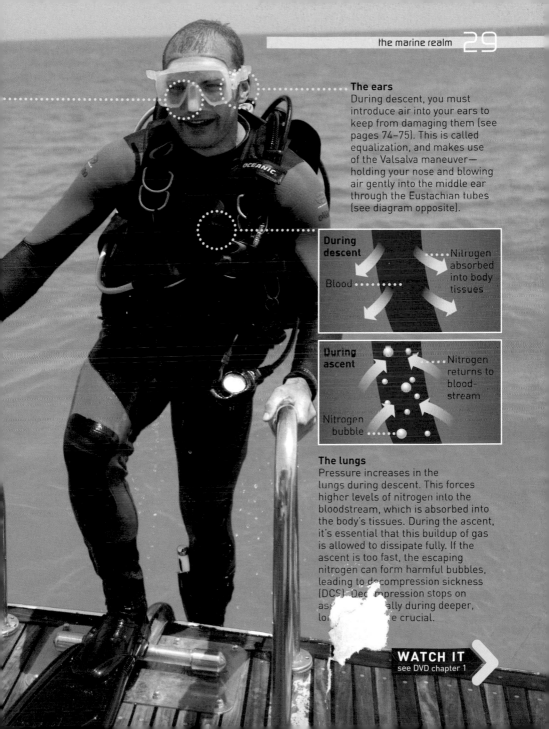

The ears
During descent, you must introduce air into your ears to keep from damaging them (see pages 74–75). This is called equalization, and makes use of the Valsalva maneuver—holding your nose and blowing air gently into the middle ear through the Eustachian tubes (see diagram opposite).

During descent

Blood

Nitrogen absorbed into body tissues

During ascent

Nitrogen returns to bloodstream

Nitrogen bubble

The lungs
Pressure increases in the lungs during descent. This forces higher levels of nitrogen into the bloodstream, which is absorbed into the body's tissues. During the ascent, it's essential that this buildup of gas is allowed to dissipate fully. If the ascent is too fast, the escaping nitrogen can form harmful bubbles, leading to decompression sickness (DCS). Decompression stops on as____ally during deeper, lo____ crucial.

WATCH IT
see DVD chapter 1

go get the basics

coming up...

Dive gear: 34–49

Diving equipment can seem intimidating at first, but it's actually surprisingly straightforward. Whether aimed at the amateur or professional diver, the principle is the same: to deliver air to a diver, and provide a safe and comfortable diving experience.

Training and safety: 50–57

From achieving a basic level of fitness to locating an authorized dive operator, safety is always the number-one consideration. In this section, find out what you need to know before you go diving.

Cylinder
The cylinder straps onto your BCD jacket and attaches to the regulator first stage.

essential gear

There are several core items of equipment that must be worn for recreational diving. You can find out about individual items of gear on the following pages, but here is the basic gear configuration for a recreational dive in tropical waters.

If you are learning to dive in colder, temperate conditions, you should wear a full-length wetsuit or drysuit (see pages 36–37), and consider wearing a hood and gloves for insulation. In addition to the items shown here, you may also require a flashlight, if visibility is poor, and a surface marker buoy so you can be more easily located by the surface vessel.

Buoyancy compensation device (BCD)
The BCD is worn like a jacket and helps control your buoyancy in the water.

Weights
Weights, often carried on a weight belt, counteract the buoyancy of your exposure suit, helping you descend.

Knife
A sharp knife, safely carried on the lower leg, is a useful tool.

Mask
Forming an airtight seal with your face, your mask allows your eyes to focus underwater.

BCD controls
Simple controls, found at the end of the BCD's hose, are used to inflate and deflate the jacket.

Regulator second stage
This is your main breathing device. An alternate air supply is delivered via the "octopus."

Dive computer
A dive computer, worn on the wrist, enables you to monitor the depth and duration of your dive.

Gauge console
The gauge console attaches to a regulator hose and shows air pressure and depth.

Fins
A good pair of fins will aid your propulsion through the water.

Exposure suit
A shortie wetsuit provides adequate protection for diving in tropical waters.

Bootees
Neoprene bootees will protect your feet during a dive.

exposure suits

The need to retain heat is one of your most important considerations when diving. Only when the water temperature reaches 90°F (32°C)—the same temperature as the surface of your skin—will your body cease to lose heat during a dive.

Water conducts heat away from the body approximately 25 times faster than air. For this reason, a good dive suit, technically known as an "exposure suit," can mean the difference between an enjoyable dive and a miserable afternoon spent shivering on a boat.

The table below outlines the recommended type and thickness of exposure suit to be worn in a variety of water temperatures.

Water temp.	Suit type	Suit thickness
32–50°F (0–10°C)	Drysuit	7–10mm
52–68°F (11–20°C)	Drysuit or full-length wetsuit	5–7mm
70–77°F (21–25°C)	Full-length wetsuit	3–5mm
79–86°F (26–30°C)	Shortie wetsuit or none	3–5mm

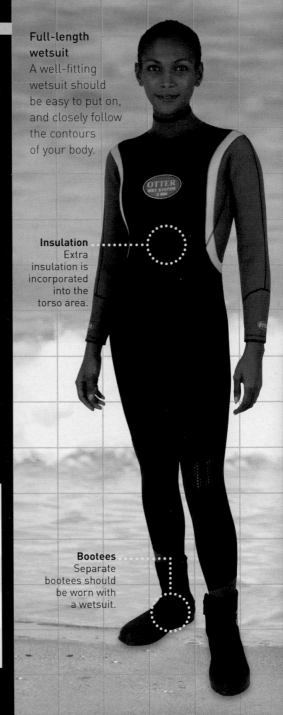

Full-length wetsuit
A well-fitting wetsuit should be easy to put on, and closely follow the contours of your body.

Insulation
Extra insulation is incorporated into the torso area.

Bootees
Separate bootees should be worn with a wetsuit.

How wetsuits work

A wetsuit works on the simple principle of trapping a layer of water between the suit and skin. This is then warmed up by the diver's body heat during the course of a dive. It is essential that a wetsuit fits well, as any circulation of water can chill a diver very quickly. Suits are made of a synthetic rubber called neoprene, which has thermal properties.

How drysuits work

Drysuits use a layer of trapped air as insulation and come in two forms: membrane and neoprene. A membrane suit acts as a tough barrier between the diver and the water and is designed to be worn with a thermal undersuit. Neoprene drysuits rely on the thermal properties of the neoprene itself and usually only require a thin undersuit.

Neoprene drysuit

Drysuit use requires additional training, as the introduction of air can adversely affect a diver's buoyancy.

Inflator valve
Drysuits require air to be added via an inflator valve and expelled via a dump valve.

Knee pads
Padding helps protect the knees.

Boots
Protective boots are integrated into the suit.

the regulator and gauges

The regulator supplies air at the correct pressure for you to breathe underwater. Complete with an integrated gauge console, it is one of the most important pieces of dive gear.

The regulator really launched mankind into the water as an independent diver. Developed by Jacques Cousteau and Emile Gagnan in 1943, the design has remained fundamentally unchanged ever since. What has changed, though, are the materials used in its manufacture. Modern regulators are made from light metal alloys and plastic compounds, and have ergonomically shaped mouthpieces for increased comfort.

Regulator first stage

The regulator's mechanism consists of two stages. The first stage (right) fits onto the cylinder and transforms compressed, high-pressure air into breathable, low-pressure air. It attaches to the tank's pillar valve using either an A-clamp, suitable for most recreational dives, or a DIN-style screw-in valve, a system popular in technical diving. In addition to supplying air to the main and reserve mouthpieces (the "second stage"), a separate hose leads from the first stage to the BCD, for inflation, and another, high-pressure hose connects to the gauge console.

Gauges

The gauge console is essential for indicating the diver's depth, and the volume of air left in the tank. Many consoles also incorporate a compass.

Pressure gauge
The submersible pressure gauge (SPG) measures the tank's air pressure in either PSI (pounds per square inch), or BAR (atmospheric pressure). It shows how much air remains in the cylinder.

Depth gauge
Measuring in either feet or meters, most depth gauges have a second needle that records the maximum depth attained during the course of the dive.

Regulator second stage

The second stage (left) fits into your mouth and delivers air as and when you breathe in. A simple tilt mechanism allows air to flow from the first stage to the second stage as you breathe in. For this reason, the regulator used to be known as the "demand valve." When you exhale, the tilt mechanism swings shut and cuts off the air supply. Your used air is then expelled into the water via exhaust vents in the mouthpiece.

cylinders

A good cylinder is fundamental to any dive and must be able to safely carry a sufficient volume of air. Cylinder design has changed little since the early days of diving.

Standard cylinders hold air at about 230 times atmospheric pressure, known as working pressure (WP), and are tested to in excess of 300 atmospheres. Typically made of either steel or aluminum, most recreational divers use a single tank. However, twin-sets (right) are often used for deep, technical dives that require lengthy decompression stops.

Cylinder sizes
Tank sizes range from tiny 6-cubic feet bottles used in rebreather kits to huge 120-cubic feet cylinders.

Standard 80-cubic feet cylinder · · · · · · ·
Made from galvanized steel, this tank is painted to protect it from corrosion.

Nitrox cylinder · · · · · · ·
Contains less nitrogen than normal air, and is used for longer dives.

13-cubic feet pony cylinder · · · · · ·
Provides an independent alternate air supply.

Suit-inflation cylinder · · · ·
The smallest tanks are used to inflate drysuits for cold-water diving.

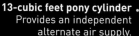

Gas mixtures

For most recreational diving, cylinders are filled with compressed air. For technical diving (see pages 144–145) a special gas mixture, such as Nitrox, may be used. This allows for longer dive times.

Pillar valve and O-ring

Air is released via a twist valve, known as a pillar valve. This may be in either an A-clamp or DIN-style configuration, for attaching to the regulator first stage (see pages 38–39). You must check the O-ring before every dive: if it's missing or damaged, the fitting won't seal properly.

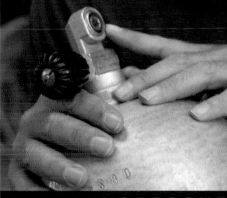

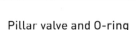

Tank markings

All cylinders have essential information marked on them, with the test date being the most important. The following details must also be shown:

- Date of manufacture

- Test pressure

- Working pressure

- Type of material (aluminum and steel have significant buoyancy differences)

buoyancy compensators

The buoyancy compensation device (BCD) is a jacket that can be filled and emptied of air to control your buoyancy both underwater and at the surface.

On descent, your wetsuit and various air spaces compress due to pressure, making you less buoyant. By introducing air to increase your buoyancy, the BCD compensates for this, and provides neutral buoyancy in much the same way as a fish's swim bladder. With practice, you will be able to fine-tune your buoyancy skills so that you can hang effortlessly in the water—essential for a good diving experience. Standard BCD jackets provide buoyancy around the shoulders, back, and under the arms, to float the diver in an upright position at the surface. Incorporated into the design are simple inflation and deflation buttons, a strap to secure the tank, large pockets, and several D-rings to secure other equipment.

Specialized jackets
Technical divers favor the high-volume "wing" style of BCD (left). This type of device has separate buoyancy bladders mounted at the back, which leaves the front of the diver uncluttered. It also offers increased lift to compensate for additional heavy equipment. Other types of BCD include those with integrated weights, and lightweight travel jackets.

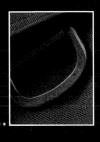

D-Ring
Used for attaching additional pieces of equipment, such as a dive flashlight, reel, or surface marker buoy (SMB).

Whistle
A safety feature, used for attracting attention at the surface of the water.

Harness release clip
Allows quick and easy donning and removal of the jacket.

Buoyancy control
The inflation and deflation controls, and oral inflator, are located at the end of a corrugated hose.

masks, snorkels, and fins

For many people, the mask, snorkel, and fins are the first introduction to diving equipment, perhaps bought on vacation for snorkeling. Despite being the most simple pieces of your gear, they play a very important role. With an ill-fitting mask, an inadequate snorkel, and the wrong type of fins, your dive would be an extremely uncomfortable experience.

Masks

Your mask should fit comfortably over your nose and face, and adhere to your face when you inhale. Modern masks are shatterproof, lightweight, extremely durable, and low volume—a smaller air space inside the mask reduces "mask squeeze" at depth.

Silcone skirt
A skirt forms an airtight seal with your face.

Lower lenses
Extra lenses enhance the downward view.

Splash-guard
A guard at the top prevents water from entering the snorkel.

Collapsible snorkel
This type of snorkel is stowed in its own case.

Snorkels

There is a bewildering array of snorkels on the market, many boasting complex venting systems and revolutionary designs. However, as long as your snorkel has a comfortable mouthpiece, a breathing tube with a wide diameter, attaches securely to your mask strap, and is easy to vent, it's the right snorkel for you!

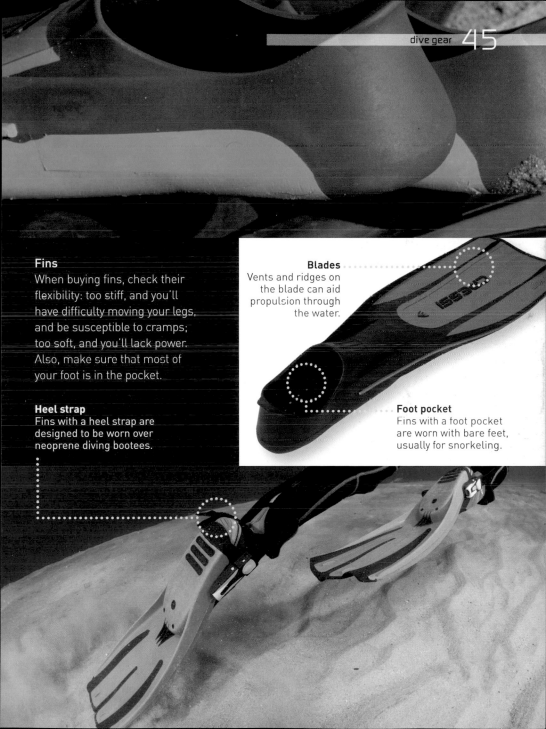

Fins

When buying fins, check their flexibility: too stiff, and you'll have difficulty moving your legs, and be susceptible to cramps; too soft, and you'll lack power. Also, make sure that most of your foot is in the pocket.

Heel strap

Fins with a heel strap are designed to be worn over neoprene diving bootees.

Blades

Vents and ridges on the blade can aid propulsion through the water.

Foot pocket

Fins with a foot pocket are worn with bare feet, usually for snorkeling.

computers and accessories

The range of diving accessories seems endless, and may be overwhelming at first, but you should resist the temptation to buy equipment for equipment's sake.

Minimalism is the order of the day when it comes to diving: additional gear creates drag, and can lead to unnecessary complications. However, certain items of gear are very helpful and, in some environments, are essential.

Flashlight
A luxury item when diving tropical sites, a good flashlight is essential in many temperate regions, whether diving during the day or night.

Dive computers

A dive computer measures the time and depth of a dive, and calculates a safe rate of ascent to avoid decompression sickness. Modern computers are worn on the wrist and offer a suite of functions to monitor every aspect of a diver's performance, both during and after the dive. Preprogrammed with decompression software, many computers have air-integrated systems that constantly monitor the diver's air consumption and work rate, adjusting the calculations accordingly. While dive computers have revolutionized safety, and certainly made life easier, they are not infallible. It's always a good idea to use traditional diving tables as a backup.

Diver's knife
Beloved of many a macho diver, there's actually no need for a dive knife to be large and heavy. Many are small, clip onto the BCD, and incorporate one-handed release mechanisms. A dive knife should be sharp enough to free a diver in case of entanglement.

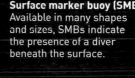

Surface marker buoy (SMB)
Available in many shapes
and sizes, SMBs indicate
the presence of a diver
beneath the surface.

Wrist computer
Many modern dive
computers are the size
of a wrist watch. Some
even have games that
can be played on long
decompression stops!

Reel
A reel may be used to
deploy an SMB, or as a
guideline for conducting
search patterns.

advanced gear

Dive gear technology continues to develop at a phenomenal rate. So much so that the diver of fifty years ago would be amazed at the gear available to his or her counterpart today.

It's true that certain pieces of equipment have stood the test of time. The most notable contender is the regulator second stage, the fundamental design of which has not changed significantly since Jacques Cousteau's time in the 1940s. However, where design principles remain unchanged, the materials from which equipment is made are constantly evolving. There is a trend toward making gear lighter, more resilient, and user-friendly. In fact, the use of strong plastics, silicones, and metal alloys means modern dive gear should last a lifetime.

Rebreather gear

Modern developments in dive equipment include the widespread use of the rebreather (below). With no exhaust bubbles, it allows for exciting encounters with often timid marine life. The concept behind rebreather diving—the recycling of exhaled air—existed well before the development of scuba equipment. But only in the last decade has the combination of computer technology and modern manufacturing techniques made rebreather diving widely accessible to the everyday diver.

Technical diving gear

For the technical diver, eager to plumb greater depths for longer periods, new dive technology has proved invaluable. Full-face masks, for example, have become more user-friendly over recent years, allowing for radio communication between divers underwater, and between divers and the surface. There have been recent developments in the application of "heads-up" LCD displays inside the diver's mask, which present key information, at the touch of a button, into the diver's line of sight. In addition, wireless transmitters attached to the regulator first stage are capable of feeding information to a diver's wrist computer, allowing for air-pressure checks on multiple tanks.

fitness for diving

To enjoy scuba diving, it's not necessary to be extremely fit, or a very strong swimmer. Diving does require a certain degree of physicality, but this varies greatly according to which form of diving you are pursuing.

A deep technical dive in temperate waters, for example, is considerably more demanding than a gentle drift over a tropical coral reef. However, studies indicate that divers who are obese, or who experience a higher level of exertion underwater, are more susceptible to decompression sickness, so it's important to maintain a basic level of fitness.

Health and fitness
Although a high level of fitness is not crucial for a safe and enjoyable dive, there are a number of considerations that will help you get the most out of your diving experiences:

- Body strength: diving equipment is relatively heavy, and a certain level of strength is needed to lift, carry, and walk in dive gear

- Aerobic conditioning: you need to be able to function effectively and efficiently for sustained periods. Running, cycling, and swimming are all great forms of exercise to achieve this.

- Hydration and diet: it is surprisingly easy to become dehydrated on a dive vessel, and many dive boats operating in deeper waters demand that divers drink fluids frequently. The ideal foods for a day's diving are those rich in complex carbohydrates, such as bananas, dried fruit, and flat breads, which release energy slowly.

learning to dive

Diving is an extremely safe sport when undertaken correctly. However, without appropriate training, it has the potential to be highly dangerous.

Taking part in a recognized training course is not only necessary for safety reasons, but it's also a legal requirement. The majority of dive operators will refuse to sell equipment, or provide air fills, to anyone unable to present an appropriate qualification. There are numerous training organizations in existence to lead you on your first, exciting steps into the world of diving.

Training organizations

Your first task is to find a training organization that offers courses relevant to your interests. PADI (Professional Association of Diving Instructors) dominates the world of recreational diving instruction, but there are many other well-respected organizations. For example, courses run by the British Sub Aqua Club (BSAC) tend to focus on the more demanding conditions encountered when diving in temperate waters.

Dive operators

Once you've identified which course best suits your needs, you need to find a local dive operator affiliated to your chosen training organization. Always research the reputation of the particular operator you're planning to use before signing up. This is the beginning of your diving adventure and should be a positive experience, providing the building block for your future diving career.

Choosing a dive course

• Find an operator you're comfortable with—you will be placing yourself totally in their hands.

• Most basic "open water" courses last about a week on a full-time basis.

• You will need to attain further qualifications before you can dive beyond certain depth limits.

picking a dive operator

The standard of dive operators around the world varies dramatically, and you should always check the credentials of the dive center or boat you are considering using. Unlike many other leisure activities undertaken on vacation, diving presents severe safety issues if an operator is run in a slipshod manner.

Happily, modern legislation means that most dive operators are well-run and perform their work to exacting standards. However, being aware of what to look for may save you from making a costly, and potentially dangerous, mistake. There are several ways to ensure that your diving experience is safe, affordable, and enjoyable.

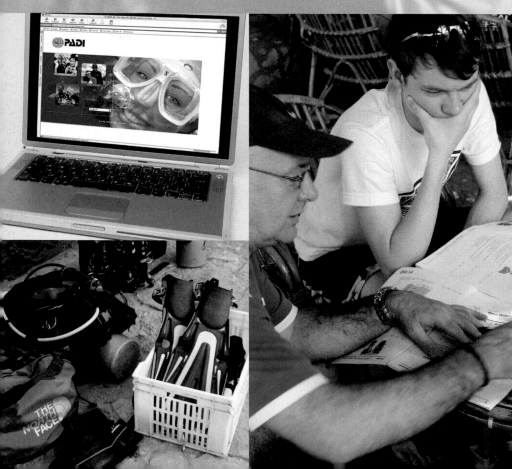

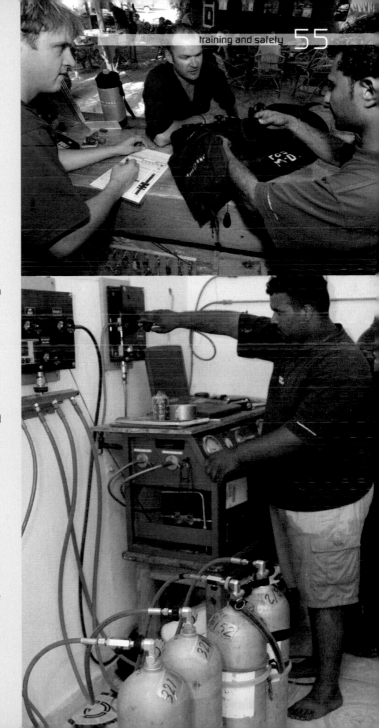

How to find a suitable dive operator

- PADI runs a website detailing registered dive operators, all of whom have passed a set of tests and are graded depending on the level of facilities on offer.

- Physically inspect the dive operator on arrival. The center should be well maintained and clean, and the minimum you should expect is courteous and professional service.

- Certificates of qualification should be clearly displayed, and the dive operator should ask to see your own qualifications before diving commences.

- Oxygen and first-aid equipment should be readily available for every dive conducted.

- The compressor room (where the cylinders are filled) should be clean, ordered, and clearly display test certificates for air quality.

dive operator safety equipment

There are certain pieces of safety equipment that are essential for diving activities to be conducted in a safe and controlled manner. Regardless of the scale or sophistication of a dive operator or vessel, these are a prerequisite, and should be considered non-negotiable when choosing a dive operator.

The presence of safety equipment is not only a crucial backup for the diver in the event of an incident, it's also an excellent measure of whether an operator is working in a professional and responsible manner. For boat and live-aboard diving, a life raft in good working order and of ample size to accommodate the divers and crew is one of the first things to look for, as well as key items of emergency gear.

Safety essentials

When choosing a dive operator, ensure the following safety equipment is present:

- Most pressure related injuries (barotraumas) require oxygen to be administered immediately. This helps flush nitrogen out of the bloodstream.

- Injuries sustained during diving are usually minor—bumps and bruises or sunburn, for example. However, a comprehensive first-aid kit should be on hand for more serious injuries.

- The boat box, which must be waterproof, should contain flares, spare parts, batteries, and tools.

- Working communication facilities must be available, so the alarm can be raised in the event of an emergency. All divers should be briefed on its use.

go get started

coming up...

Preparing to dive: 62–67

Careful preparation is essential for a safe and successful diving experience. Find out how to prepare your equipment and assemble it correctly.

Basic skills: 68–99

There are certain key skills, such as mask removal and regulator retrieval, that you must master before you can dive independently. Even experienced divers should hone these techniques periodically, and those who haven't dived for a while should revise them before embarking on a dive.

Advanced skills: 100–113

The techniques in this section, such as rescue procedures and deploying an SMB, are all slightly more advanced. Although not essential for everyday recreational diving, becoming proficient in these skills will greatly enhance your enjoyment and safety.

preparing your gear

The urge to reach the dive site and get into the water as quickly as possible can be all-consuming, but many a dive has been called off due to hasty preparation, or poorly packed equipment.

Take a few moments at home to ensure that everything is present and fully functional. It's either impossible, or unsafe, to continue with a dive if equipment is missing or malfunctioning. There's nothing worse than arriving at a site, looking out over perfect conditions, then realizing that an item of gear is hundreds of miles away at home.

a

b

c

d

Make a checklist
A simple waterproofed sheet with check boxes alongside each item of gear will help ensure all your gear makes it to the dive site.

Inspect for damage
It is always a good idea to check your gear for damage, particularly if it has been unused, or in storage, for a long time.

Fully assemble to test
Assembling your equipment to test it out is not only good practice, it will also highlight any areas of damage, or missing parts.

Turn everything on
Turning on your air at the dive site and being greeted by a cacophony of hissing hoses and spluttering regulators is disheartening—test it out first!

packing your gear

Dive gear represents a considerable investment, yet it is surprising how many divers neglect their gear, or throw items into a bag without a second thought.

Bad packing is one of the main causes of breakages and malfunctions of dive gear. As well as being expensive to repair, poorly cared-for gear can present real safety issues. There are many specialized dive bags on the market, designed specifically to transport and protect your gear. Although specialized bags may have a hard base, or be highly durable, a large, strong bag will suffice, and is often far cheaper. It must be big enough to hold your BCD, exposure suit, regulator, mask, snorkel, and fins (cylinders are usually rented on-site).

a

a Gear bag
Look for a large, strong gear bag to carry and protect your equipment in transit.

b Pack in order
Packing your gear in a specific order not only ensures nothing is left behind, but it also helps protect delicate items.

c Protect fragile items
Cushion delicate items, such as the regulator, with a wetsuit. Carry your weights or weight belt separately.

d Use hand luggage
Carry particularly sensitive gear, such as a dive computer, in hand luggage. Hand luggage is also useful for carrying additional items, such as a hat and sunscreen.

WATCH IT
see DVD chapter 2

b

c

d

assembling your gear

Your dive gear is essentially life-support equipment, so it is vital that you know how to assemble it correctly. The process of setting up your equipment is a key part of any dive, and is one of the first skills taught on any dive course. There are hard-and-fast rules that all divers must follow before entering the water.

1

How to set up your gear
Examine the cylinder to make sure the test dates are valid, the O-ring is not nicked or distorted, and the tank is in good condition. Check the BCD's clips and straps for signs of wear.

2

Secure the BCD to the cylinder using the tank band. Position it two-thirds of the way up the cylinder, so the pillar valve and first stage don't restrict your head movements when you are in the water.

3

Thoroughly inspect the hoses for damage, then attach the regulator to the tank. Don't overtighten it—the air pressure will provide a powerful seal.

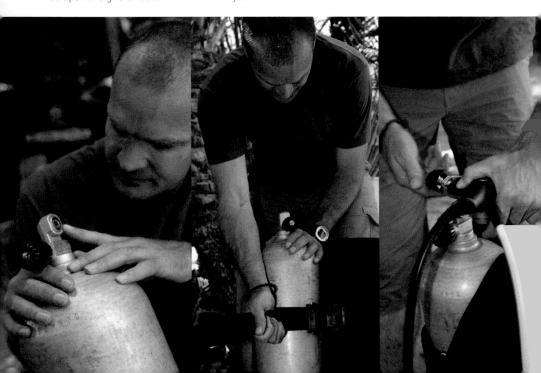

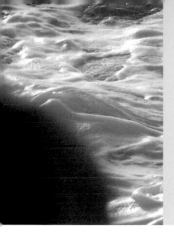

Storing your gear

If you don't intend to dive straight away, always store your gear properly in the meantime. Lie the cylinder on the ground and tuck away the gauges and regulators. Turn off the air, and purge the regulators to expel air from the hoses.

4 Clip the octopus and inflator hose to the BCD. Holding the pressure gauge away from you, slowly turn the air on all the way. Then turn it back half a turn.

5 Make sure there is enough air in the cylinder for your dive, and breathe through your main and octopus regulators in turn. Check the quality and delivery of the air supply.

6 Inflate and deflate your BCD to check that it works correctly. You will repeat this exercise during your predive buddy checks (see pages 68–69)

WATCH IT
see DVD chapter 2

the buddy system

Diving with a buddy is essential. Your buddy supports you (and you support your buddy) during every phase of a dive, from the initial planning and checking of your equipment, to providing safety support during the dive itself.

This support begins with the buddy checks, which are made once you are fully outfitted, just prior to your dive. In addition to being a crucial safety measure, the shared experience of diving with a buddy is bound to increase your enjoyment.

1

Performing buddy checks
Check your buddy's air supply, ensuring it's turned on, and that both the main regulator second stage and octopus are delivering air correctly. Check the air pressure, and that the octopus is readily accessible.

2

Depress the inflation and deflation buttons on the BCD's air hose. Check that air is entering and leaving the BCD correctly, and that the jacket fully inflates and deflates.

3 If you're carrying your weights on a weight belt, check that it's right-hand release. Ensure that the weight belt or weight pouches are securely fitted. Make sure that either you or your buddy can easily remove them in the event of an emergency.

4 Ensure that the clips supporting your buddy's gear are secure. Check that either you or your buddy can unclip and remove key items of equipment quickly.

WATCH IT
see DVD chapter 2

5 Run through the hand signals you will be using during the dive to ensure they are understood. Check you have all the necessary additional items of gear (such as a flashlight or SMB), and that they are functioning correctly.

6 Finally, check that you have both agreed on a plan for the dive, and understand your goals. If you are both happy to begin your dive, give the OK signal.

entering the water

continued >

There are four widely used methods used by scuba divers to enter the water: the giant stride, the backward roll, seated, and shore entries.

The giant stride is used to enter the water from a platform above the water, such as the dive platform of a large vessel. The backward roll is used when entering from a smaller boat or RIB (rigid inflatable boat). The seated entry can also be used from a small boat or RIB, as well as from the side of a pool, and shore entry is for dives just off the coast.

1

Giant stride entry
Adopt the entry position and check that your entry point is clear and that the water is deep enough. Take a large step forward.

2

Look forward, not down, and make the stride high and wide, splayed-scissor fashion, to prevent the blade of your leading fin from hitting the surface.

Entry position

Remember to half-inflate your BCD before you enter the water. This will ensure that you are buoyant enough to stay at the surface after entry. Place the regulator in your mouth and put on your mask. For the giant stride and backward roll entry, cover the mask and regulator with your hand to keep them in place during the maneuver. Place your other hand around the front of your body to secure any trailing equipment. Maintain this position until you are fully in the water.

3 Hold the splayed-scissor position of your legs on splashdown. This will cushion the impact, and help keep you at the surface.

4 Once in the water, turn to face the dive marshal and signal that everything is OK. Then, swim away from the entry point to clear the way for other divers.

WATCH IT
see DVD chapter 3

entering the water (continued)

Shore entry

The key to entering the water from the shore is that you and your buddy physically support each other, since entering the water in full dive gear over an uneven seabed can be difficult. The best way to steady yourself is to place an arm around your buddy's shoulders as you walk. You can choose to walk in either backward or forward. If the surf is reasonably large, it is easier to wear your fins, place your regulator in your mouth, and walk backward. Glance back as you progress, and brace yourself against the waves. If the surf is relatively calm, you may decide to carry your fins and walk in forward (it is difficult to move forward while wearing your fins), putting them on only when you reach deeper water.

WATCH IT
see DVD chapter 3

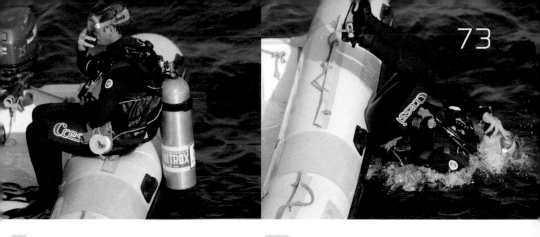

1 Backward roll entry

The backward roll is the standard form of entry from smaller boats. Adopt the entry position by putting the regulator in your mouth, placing one hand over the mask and regulator, and keeping your other hand across the front of your body.

2

Ensure that the water behind you is clear of obstacles or other divers. On the signal from the dive marshal, roll backward, and maintain the position of your hands to keep any trailing equipment out of the way.

1 Seated entry

This form of entry is used in a pool, from a platform just above water level, or from a RIB (as pictured). Turn from your waist and place both hands to one side of your body, ready to take your weight.

2

Pivot your body around, using your hands to support you, so that you turn to face the side of the boat while easing yourself into the water.

making your descent

The descent is the moment when you fully commit to a dive, and there are a number of procedures you should follow for a safe and controlled descent.

Before you begin your descent, make sure you are clear from any obstacles. In particular, be aware of dive boats, which should move away from divers in the water, or remain static so the divers can swim away on the surface.

Many training organizations advise checking the time before you descend (so you can monitor the duration of your dive and avoid decompression sickness), although modern dive computers automatically record the time.

At about 10 ft (3 m) below the surface, perform a bubble check to make sure no air is leaking from your buddy's gear. If you or your buddy spot a significant leak, return to the surface immediately.

If you find you don't descend when your BCD is fully deflated, return to the boat for extra weights.

How to descend safely
Meet up with your buddy on the surface and give the OK signal. This ensures you are both ready, and that neither of you will be left struggling on the surface, or feel pressured into descending too soon.

When you are in position, confirm your intention to begin the descent immediately by giving each other the "let's descend" signal.

2 If you are breathing through your snorkel, now is the time to remove it and place the regulator in your mouth. This may sound obvious, but it's actually a surprisingly common oversight.

3 Orientate toward your objective, and then face your buddy. This ensures you know where to aim for during the descent, and where your buddy is located should you become separated or disorientated on the way down.

WATCH IT
see DVD chapter 3

5 Raise your BCD's deflation and inflation hose, and depress the deflation button. As you let out the air, you should start to descend. Hold your nose with your other hand, ready to clear, or "equalize," your ears.

6 Equalize your ears as soon as you start to descend, and clear them continuously throughout the descent. If you have trouble, or feel pain, ascend a little and try again. Remember to conduct a bubble check at about 10 ft (3 m).

using hand signals

Communicating effectively underwater is a challenge as old as diving itself. Although speech can be heard if one diver positions his or her regulator against the other's ear and shouts, this is far from practical.

Hand signals are the accepted means of communication between divers, and, with occasional local variations, are standard throughout the diving world. Certain diving specializations, such as photographic shoots, may require specific hand signals, and the predive briefing should always include a discussion on the hand signals to be used.

OK/Are you OK?
Form an "O" with your thumb and forefinger. Point other fingers up.

Something is wrong
With your palm facing down, tilt your hand from side to side.

Up/Let's ascend
Point your thumb straight up, clenching your fingers in a fist.

Down/Let's go down
Point your thumb down, and clench your fingers in a fist.

Stop
Present the flat of your hand, palm out, to halt buddy or other divers.

1,500 PSI (100 BAR) left
Form a T-shape with your hands to indicate 1,500 PSI of air remaining.

750 PSI (50 BAR) left
Make a fist, palm facing out, to indicate 750 PSI of air remaining.

I am out of air
Make a horizontal chopping motion across the base of your neck.

Slow down
Move palms slowly down together, pivoting at the elbows.

Stay/Move together
Bring your forefingers together, so they are side by side and touching.

Stay at this depth
Hold both hands horizontally and move one over the other.

Watch/Look
Point at your eyes, then at the subject you want other divers to look at.

I am cold
Hold yourself, with both arms crossed, to indicate chill.

I can't clear my ears
Point at your ear to indicate you are having difficulty equalizing.

Feeling breathless
If you are feeling out of breath, and need to rest briefly, use the flat of your hand to mimic your chest rising and falling.

mask clearing and regulator retrieval

Two key diving skills are the ability to clear your mask if it fills with water, and retrieve your regulator if it is knocked from your mouth. For the beginner, practicing these techniques can feel unnatural. Some trainee divers find mask clearing particularly offputting, as it requires careful coordination of your breathing between your mouth and nose.

Both techniques are essential for a safe and enjoyable dive. Mask clearing is a particularly useful skill, since you will need to remove small amounts of water on most dives. When you perform the regulator retrieval drills, always blow a small, steady stream of bubbles from your mouth whenever the regulator is removed. This ensures that you never create a closed air space (through holding your breath), which can lead to lung expansion injuries.

1 Regulator retrieval—sweep method
Adopt an upright position on the seabed, leaning slightly to the right. Start with your right arm next to your thigh, raise your hand, and sweep it forward in an arc.

2 Continue sweeping your right arm forward until you make contact with the regulator hose. Bring your left hand up to collect the hose, and place the regulator in your mouth.

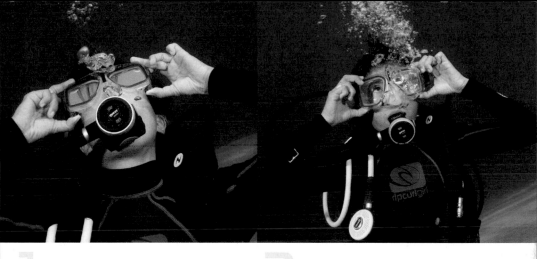

Mask clearing

1 Kneel on the seabed and adopt an upright position. Tilt your head back slightly so that you're facing toward the surface.

2 Lift the lower edge of your mask away from your face, either by pressing on the top edge or by lifting up the bottom edge. As you do this, exhale through your nostrils to force out the water. If any water remains, repeat the process.

3 Once the regulator is in place, you must exhale before breathing in. This purges the regulator of water. If you don't have enough breath left, depress the purge button on the regulator instead.

Regulator retrieval—hose method

An alternative method of retrieving a lost regulator is the hose method. Remembering to blow a small stream of bubbles from your mouth for as long as the regulator is removed, reach behind you until you find the regulator first stage, which is attached to the pillar valve at the top of the cylinder. Then, trace the length of the hose down to the regulator second stage, and return the mouthpiece to your mouth. As with the sweep method, purge water from the regulator before you take a breath.

WATCH IT >
see DVD chapter 3

buoyancy control

Good buoyancy control means achieving neutral buoyancy underwater so you neither float nor sink. It begins with being correctly weighted at the surface, and involves letting small amounts of air in and out of your BCD until you can maintain your position in the water with the minimum of effort.

Aside from emergency and self-rescue skills, buoyancy is the most important diving skill to master. Good buoyancy control leads to reduced air consumption, and increased safety during the dive and on ascent (especially during decompression stops). It takes time and experience to master, but good buoyancy control makes diving far more enjoyable.

Correct weighting

To achieve good buoyancy, you first need to be correctly weighted. A simple buoyancy check on the surface is always advisable. With your BCD deflated, and holding a normal breath, you should float at eye level with the surface of the water.

WATCH IT
see DVD chapter 3

Good buoyancy

One of the key benefits of good buoyancy control is that you will have less impact on the marine environment, and be better able to approach marine animals. Coral, for example, is extremely delicate and can be easily damaged by physical contact. Achieving good buoyancy requires extensive practice, and there are certain drills you can perform to help you fine tune your skills (see pages 82–83).

Poor buoyancy

Common faults with buoyancy control include using corrective fin kicks to maintain position in the water, and trying to compensate for poor buoyancy by holding the body in a sloping position. Holding the wrong profile can lead to kicking up sand and silt (right), which may impair visibility. Poor buoyancy control during the descent can lead to the diver not being in an upright position, and not holding the BCD hose straight, which may make it difficult to dump air.

perfecting buoyancy control

Once you have attained a basic level of buoyancy control, there are a number of drills you can practice to improve your buoyancy skills.

As you begin to master buoyancy control, you will notice a reduction in your rate of air consumption, and will begin to enjoy your diving experiences more fully.

Practice fin pivots and the hover, remembering never to hold your breath. They are best practiced in confined water, such as a pool, or in a sheltered environment.

More advanced drills include the horizontal hover, the nose stand, and the use of hoops and bars. The horizontal hover involves hovering close to the bottom, and sculling back and forth, with no part of your body or equipment touching the floor. The nose stand is an advanced maneuver that involves holding a vertical, head-down position, and inching toward an object on the bottom. Hoops suspended in the water, or a bar just above the bottom, can also be used to create an obstacle course that requires subtle changes in buoyancy.

The hover
Move into an upright, cross-legged position in midwater. Grasp the tips of your fins with your hands and try to maintain this position. If you start to rise, breathe more lightly. If you start to fall, breathe more deeply. A more advanced version of the drill is to perform another skill simultaneously. For example, rather than holding your fins, you could attempt to deploy a delayed surface marker buoy while you hover.

Fin pivots
Maintain a horizontal position, close to the seafloor, with your legs apart. Your fins should touch the bottom and act as a hinge. Spread out your arms, holding the BCD hose in your hand.

WATCH IT
see DVD chapter 3 >

2 Breathe in gently and feel your upper body begin to rise. Keep your fin tips on the bottom for stability, and stop breathing in when you reach an angle of about 45°.

3 Slowly breathe out again until your body begins to fall. Before you hit the bottom, begin to inhale again. Repeat this process until you feel completely in control of your buoyancy.

trim and finning

Trim is your posture as you move through the water, and finning is the kicking action you use for propulsion.

The ideal trim for most diving environments is with the head slightly up, to prevent you from craning your neck as you look ahead. However, a head-down position may be preferable if you are diving over a delicate reef. This elevates the legs, and reduces the likelihood of your fins brushing the reef as you kick.

Basic finning skills are taught on most diving courses, although there are a number of techniques—and different fin types—that can be used in different environments.

How to achieve good trim
Achieving good trim involves holding the right posture in the water, and positioning your weights and equipment correctly. Having good trim will improve your buoyancy control.

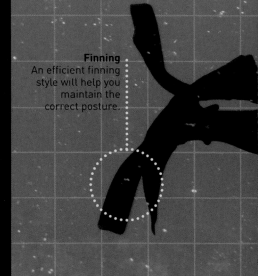

Finning
An efficient finning style will help you maintain the correct posture.

Moving underwater
The standard finning technique is the swimmer kick. It requires straight legs, reasonably rigid ankles, and a steady, firm kick to drive you forward. A common mistake with this kick is to bend the knees and keep the toes up, which results in an inefficient "bicycling" technique. For environments with a fine substrate, the frog kick or flutter kick should be used instead. The power in these strokes is directed away from the seafloor, allowing you to progress without disturbing the substrate.

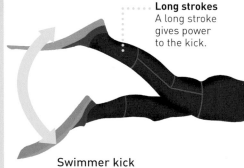

Long strokes
A long stroke gives power to the kick.

Swimmer kick
Lock your legs and kick from the hips with long strokes to exploit the power in your thigh muscles.

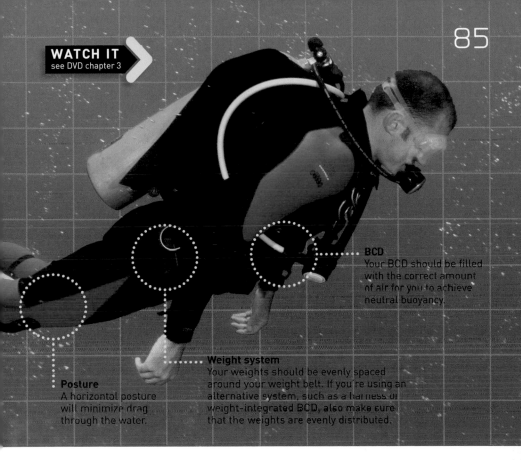

WATCH IT
see DVD chapter 3

BCD
Your BCD should be filled with the correct amount of air for you to achieve neutral buoyancy.

Weight system
Your weights should be evenly spaced around your weight belt. If you're using an alternative system, such as a harness or weight-integrated BCD, also make sure that the weights are evenly distributed.

Posture
A horizontal posture will minimize drag through the water.

Angled fins
The water is forced behind you as your fins come together.

Powerful downstroke
The power of the stroke comes from the downward movement.

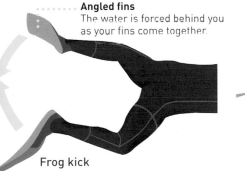

Frog kick

Spread your legs, bring up your knees, angle the bottoms of your fins behind you, and bring them together in an arc.

Flutter kick

Bend your knees for a shorter kick, and keep your hips fairly static. The stroke ends with your legs straightened.

using an alternate air source

You should always have access to an alternate air source (AAS) while underwater. Since you will be diving with a buddy, this usually takes the form of their reserve regulator second stage— known as an "octopus."

Knowing how to signal to your buddy that you want to use their octopus, and coordinating its use, is a crucial scuba-diving skill. Buddy breathing, the sharing of a single air supply between two divers, is another key technique.

You should also be equipped with an octopus that your buddy can use, and that you can use if your main second stage malfunctions. However, as the octopus runs off the same first stage as your primary air source, it will be of no use if the first stage fails or you run out of gas. For a backup air source to be truly reliable, it should be independent. If any aspect of the primary air source fails, the reserve may then be used without risk. Many experienced divers choose to use a smaller pony bottle, with an independent regulator.

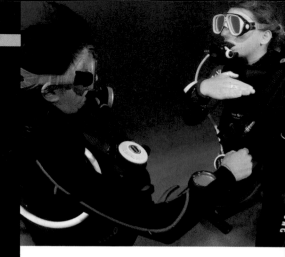

1 Using your buddy's octopus
If you want to use your buddy's octopus, first signal that you are low, or out of air. Make a horizontal chopping action across the base of your neck.

Reserve air supply
The octopus is often fluorescent yellow in color. This makes it highly visible underwater, and distinguishes it from the main air supply.

2 Your buddy (the donor diver) should offer their octopus by turning their body and indicating its position. Place the AAS in your mouth, and purge it before you breathe in.

3 Once you are breathing normally, establish physical contact with each other and signal that you are OK. The donor diver should initiate a controlled ascent (see pages 90–91).

How to buddy breathe

Buddy breathing involves the passage of a single regulator between two divers. Although it isn't taught by every training organization—due to the widespread use of the octopus—it is, nonetheless, a very useful technique. The donor diver carefully controls the movement of their regulator second stage, with each diver taking two breaths at a time. This is very much an emergency procedure, and should only be used to extract a diver to the surface. Any out-of-air situation is highly stressful and potentially hazardous, even for experienced divers, and events may not follow such a neat set of stages.

WATCH IT
see DVD chapter 4

weight belt removal and replacement

Removing and replacing your weight belt is a crucial skill, and is taught on every basic diving course. You may need to remove and adjust it for comfort reasons, to add or remove a weight for better buoyancy, or to disentangle equipment. You must be able to perform the maneuvers in a safe and controlled manner.

Safety considerations

Ensure that your weight belt is secured for a right-hand release, and always keep a firm grip on the weight belt as you perform the techniques on these pages. Dropping your weight belt while removing, adjusting, or replacing it can have serious safety implications. Losing your weights during the course of a dive means that you will become positively buoyant, and could make a fast, uncontrolled ascent—an extremely hazardous situation. You should only deliberately dump your weight belt in an emergency, and as a last resort, if you need to ascend quickly to the surface.

WATCH IT
see DVD chapter 3

1 Removing your weight belt

Signal to your buddy that you are performing the drill, then sink to the seafloor. Remove all the air from your BCD to establish negative buoyancy. Grasp the loose end of the belt in your right hand.

Replacing your weight belt

To replace your weight belt, grasp the loose end in your right hand, place the belt next to your right hip, and roll your body into it. Once the belt is in position—a process that may take a certain amount of adjustment—you should fasten it securely. Only when you are sure that the buckle is fastened properly should you let go of the belt.

2 Maintaining a firm grip, undo the buckle by pulling the loose end to the right. Hold the buckle against your body with your left hand, and move your right hand just behind the buckle. Now pull the loose end free with your right hand.

3 Once you have slid the belt off, you can make any necessary adjustments. To alter the position of the weights, it's good practice to sit on the seafloor and drape the belt over your knee. Keep a firm hold on the belt throughout.

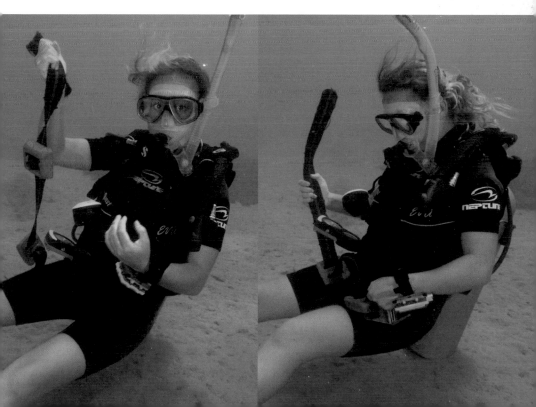

making your ascent

A controlled ascent is vital in order to avoid decompression sickness or potential obstacles on the surface. Many of the incidents that happen when diving do so during the ascent, in much the same way as mountaineering accidents often occur as the climbers descend from a peak. It is vital to guard against complacency: the dive isn't over until you are out of the water. The key to a controlled ascent is good buoyancy control, as the air in your body and equipment expands as you ascend, increasing your buoyancy and rate of ascent.

1 Performing a controlled ascent
Once you decide to ascend, orientate yourself with your buddy and clearly signal your intention. Wait for your buddy to return the thumbs-up signal.

2 To begin the ascent, establish neutral buoyancy and gently fin upward. Holding up the BCD's hose, slowly and steadily dump air from your BCD. Raise your other arm above your head and maintain a steady breathing rate.

WATCH IT
see DVD chapter 4

3 Your rate of ascent should be approximately 60 ft (18 m) per minute—as a rule of thumb, never ascend faster than your smallest exhaled bubbles. Whenever possible, make a decompression safety stop at 20 ft (6 m). Wait for three minutes before commencing the final phase of the ascent.

4 After your safety stop, continue your ascent very slowly, allowing a full minute for the last 10 ft (3 m). Scan the area before you reach the surface and listen out for boat traffic. As you surface, use your raised arm for protection against overhead obstacles. Fully inflate your BCD to establish positive buoyancy, and give a clear "OK" signal to the boat.

Exhale throughout the procedure
It is vital that you breathe out during the ascent. Holding your breath can damage your lungs, as the air inside you will expand as you ascend.

emergency ascents

The Controlled Emergency Swimming Ascent (CESA) is an emergency procedure that should only be performed in extreme circumstances. It requires the diver to look up, reach up, and swim up, and is used in an out-of-air situation if buddy assistance is not available.

If a dive is correctly supervised, conducted responsibly, and proper checks are performed, the emergency ascent shouldn't be necessary. Most divers will never need to perform the procedure in a real-life situation.

The CESA is designed so that you can extract yourself from depth to the surface at the best possible speed with the minimum risk of injury. However, it is a hazardous maneuver, and should only be performed as a last resort.

Essential safety tips

• Exhale throughout the ascent. Most training organizations teach divers to make an audible "aaahhhh" sound, ensuring the airway is open and exhalation is taking place.

• As you ascend through the water column, keep the regulator second stage in your mouth. Any air left in the cylinder will expand as the pressure decreases. There may be enough air remaining for a breath or two before you reach the surface.

• Control the speed of your ascent by using the inflation and deflation buttons on the BCD hose. Remember that air will expand in your BCD and should be vented periodically to prevent an uncontrolled ascent.

Look up
As you ascend, look up, and look around you. It's vital that you are constantly aware of the surrounding environment, and that nothing, including other divers, impedes your ascent.

Reach up
Raise your arm above your head. If there is an obstruction overhead, you can push it out of the way with your free hand (the hand not holding the BCD hose).

WATCH IT
see DVD chapter 4

Swim up
Using a swimmer kick (see pages 84–85), try to maintain a normal rate of ascent of 60 ft (18 m) per minute. Exhale slowly and steadily as you ascend to prevent lung expansion injuries.

surfacing

Your dive is not over until you are fully out of the water, and you must be acutely aware of your surroundings as you break the surface. Surface traffic—particularly in regions heavily used by recreational boats—can be dangerous.

Although any respectable dive boat will fly an A-flag (indicating that diving is taking place, and that other boats should steer clear), many boat users are ignorant of the rules, or even choose to ignore them. In the latter stages of your ascent, it is crucial to carefully observe the surface and make your presence known to any approaching boats when you are on the surface.

Exiting the water

- To exit onto a hard boat, swim to the ladder and hold onto the bottom. Be careful in swell since it will move in the water. Remove your fins at the base of the ladder and hand them up to the boat, along with any small items of gear. You can then climb the ladder still wearing the rest of your gear.

- To exit onto a sandy beach, swim to shore with your buddy, wearing your fins for as long as possible (removing them too early can be dangerous if you're swept off your feet).

- To exit onto a rocky shore, find the easiest route back onto the rocks, again wearing your fins for as long as possible.

Signaling to the boat

As soon as you break the surface, establish positive buoyancy by fully inflating your BCD. Then, if you are diving from a boat, signal to the vessel to indicate that you are OK. The dive marshal will return your signal.

WATCH IT
see DVD chapter 4

breaking down your gear

After a dive, resist the temptation to simply shrug-off your dive gear, even though this is the moment when memories are freshest—and stories tallest!

Most divers, particularly those with more experience, only consider a dive to be truly over when their gear has been rinsed, dried, and stored away. This is a sensible philosophy that helps ensure many years of use from costly items of dive gear. The process of breaking down your gear is essentially the same as assembling it, but in reverse.

1 How to break down gear
Turn off the air and purge the regulators to expel air under pressure from the hoses. Remove the first stage from the cylinder's pillar valve.

2 If the regulator first stage is difficult to unscrew, there may be air left in the system. Purge the regulators again by pressing the purge button on each mouthpiece.

3 Dry the first-stage dust cap with a good blow, or a blast of air from the cylinder. The noise of this is piercing, so warn nearby divers first.

Rinse with fresh water

When you have broken down your gear, clean it with fresh water in a rinse tank, or using a hose. Saltwater is extremely corrosive, and dried salt crystals are sharp enough to scratch or pierce your gear, so be thorough. Never depress the regulator's purge button when in the rinse tank, since water may enter the delicate system.

4 Attach the dust cap to the seat on the first stage and unclip all the hoses and attachments from the BCD. You can now remove the BCD from the cylinder by undoing the buckle on the strap and sliding the jacket upward.

5 Invert the BCD and press the deflator button to drain away the saltwater. It's a good idea to refill the BCD with fresh water and drain it again to rinse out the inside of the jacket.

WATCH IT
see DVD chapter 4

Once you have disassembled your gear post dive, make sure it is rinsed, and correctly stored. This is especially important if you do not intend to dive again for a while. You may need to carry out basic maintenance, such as cleaning or O-ring replacement, but for more advanced work always use a registered technician. Servicing by an unqualified person is a safety risk, and invalidates your warranty.

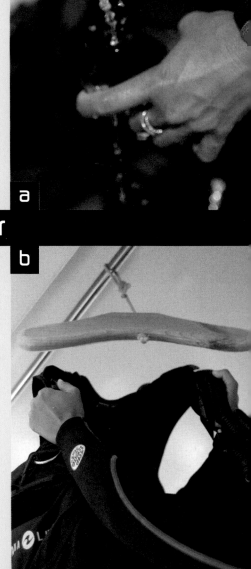

a

b

caring for your gear

⊙ Rinse well with fresh water
Use fresh water to rinse your gear after every dive. This helps keep it free of mud and sand, and is especially important when diving in saltwater. If left, salt will corrode the metal parts of your equipment.

b Dry thoroughly
Give your gear time to dry out fully. Packing wet gear can lead to deterioration, as well as some colorful odors when it's unpacked later! Find a location out of direct sunlight and orally inflate the BCD for quicker drying.

c Hang the regulator carefully
It's important to hang the regulator correctly while it dries, ensuring that no strain is placed on the hoses where they attach to the first stage.

d Store properly
Pack your equipment in a cool place where moisture won't accumulate. Make sure it is not compressed and that there are no kinks or twists in the hoses.

c

d

Basic maintenance and repair

Some basic gear maintenance can be attempted, and is a good precautionary measure against wear and tear. Most regulators and BCDs come with spare parts as standard, including detailed instructions on how to attach them. However, for more complicated repairs, you should seek professional help. This is especially important where life-support equipment is concerned, such as the regulator.

- The start of the diving season is an essential time to perform basic gear maintenance, such as replacing worn parts. Equipment is likely to have languished in storage, unused, for a long period of time.

- When inspecting your gear, look out for wear and tear in load-bearing straps and buckles, cracked O-rings, leaky hoses, and corrosion on metal surfaces and joints.

- Most divers carry a simple tool gear on every dive trip. It's often all that's needed to solve a problem, and avoid the disappointment of an abandoned dive. Your tool gear should contain lubricants (such as silicone gel), Allen wrenches, spare O-rings, pliers, wrenches, tape, tie-wraps, and a range of straps and buckles.

navigation

Underwater navigation is an essential skill if you want to move beyond simple guided dives. Being able to use a compass and read the natural signs of underwater topography will allow you to move independently, explore new areas, dive safely at unknown sites, and practice search and salvage techniques.

Orientating yourself underwater can be confusing, and every experienced diver has become lost at some stage. To help keep you from losing your way, familiarize yourself with the main reasons why divers become disorientated:

• Sound travels much faster underwater, making it difficult to locate the origin of familiar noises (such as the boat's engine).

• Currents and swell can buffet a diver, leading to changes in orientation during a dive.

• Limited visibility and similar underwater topography (such as kelp forests or rocky reefs) can easily become confusing.

WATCH IT
see DVD chapter 5

a

Natural navigation
This relies on the diver orienting
themselves to natural features, such as reef
formations, or manmade features, such as
buoy lines. Orientating toward your dive
buddy, or a distinctive feature, provides
a clear sense of direction at the bottom.

Compass navigation
This is the only guaranteed way to travel
in the correct direction. Beware of lateral
currents, which may cause you to travel
sideways as well as forward. The compass
should be held flat, orientated to the center
line of the body.

b

using an smb

A surface marker buoy (SMB) is a float that alerts surface traffic to the fact that diving is taking place in the area.

For recreational water users, impact with boats is one of the major causes of injury. An SMB warns other water users to steer clear, and gives visible notice to the support vessel that the diver is in the final stages of their ascent. It can also act as a guideline for making a safe ascent.

Deploying an SMB is a prudent measure in virtually every diving environment, particularly during a decompression stop. The major exception to this rule is when diving in overhead environments, such as ice diving, where there is no clear path to the surface.

1 **How to deploy an SMB**
Unclip the SMB from its storage position. Make sure you never deploy an SMB while it is attached to your equipment.

2 Carefully unfurl the SMB, and check that the line is not tangled or caught on your equipment.

3 Use your octopus or BCD hose to add a little air to the SMB. Add only enough to unfurl it in an upright position.

WATCH IT
see DVD chapter 4

4 Once the SMB is upright, it can be inflated. Only fill it about half full with air before deploying it: the air inside will expand as it rises.

5 Release the SMB to the surface. If the reel snags at any point, let go of the SMB immediately to prevent an uncontrolled ascent.

6 The SMB should be clearly visible to the support vessel. By the time you surface, your boat cover should be on its way to recover you.

night diving

A reef dived after dark bears little resemblance to the same reef dived during the day. An entirely new community of animals emerges to hunt, feed, and forage, and even those met during daylight hours behave differently at night.

Night diving requires a particular set of skills and additional equipment. The very fact that it's dark can lead to problems in orientation, communication with a dive buddy, and safety support throughout the dive. A good flashlight is essential, although a surprising amount can be seen by switching it off. If the Moon is strong, your eyes will quickly adjust to the gloom, and without the intrusive glare of a flashlight, many marine animals will simply go about their evening's business, unperturbed by your presence.

a

b

WATCH IT
see DVD chapter 5

Use a good flashlight
A good flashlight is essential, and many divers carry a backup. Light sticks also provide alternative illumination, and different-colored sticks can be used to identify individual divers, or key features such as the anchor line.

Show respect to marine life
Marine life should be treated with great respect on a night dive. This is a time of predatory activity on the reef, and a quiet approach, with minimum lights, can lead to more rewarding nighttime encounters.

Signal with care
Wave your flashlight to attract your buddy's attention, but never shine it in their face as you'll dazzle them. Direct the beam onto your hand as you signal, or trace shapes, such as a large circle for the OK sign, onto the seabed.

Deploy an SMB
Use a surface marker buoy to maintain contact with your boat cover throughout your dive. A good tip to ensure that you are easily located at the surface is to shine a flashlight into the inflated SMB.

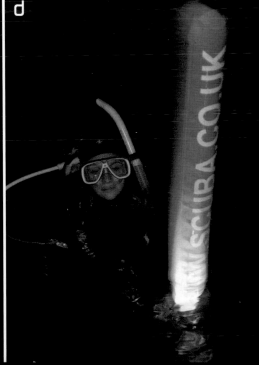

drift diving

Drift diving involves using the currents and tidal movements of the sea for propulsion through the water. This form of diving offers some of the best opportunities to view large marine animals and spectacular reefs.

Drift diving also means that you can cover greater distances than on a standard dive, with the additional advantage that very little energy is expended en route. It can be a highly rewarding form of diving, akin to flying as you bank and turn, while reefs and walls pass beneath.

There are a number of situations to be wary of when drift diving. The diver is at the whim of the current, and good buoyancy control, boat support, and diver briefings are essential. Any current faster than one knot will carry you wherever it happens to be going (you are essentially plankton in these circumstances!), and currents don't always move laterally. The underwater topography creates occasional down currents, an unpleasant sensation for the diver. Avoid areas where fish are pointing directly at the surface while maintaining their position in the water column, since this indicates the presence of a down current.

WATCH IT
see DVD chapter 5

Dive briefing
Drift diving demands extensive briefing, and a certain level of experience in those taking part. All divers must be aware of the underwater conditions, and be experienced enough to have good buoyancy control.

Surface marker buoy
The use of an SMB is essential when drift diving. The support vessel needs a clear reference point to identify the location of the divers throughout the dive.

Marine-life behavior
Observe the behavior of the marine life around you. Fish will orientate themselves to the prevailing current, and mass at points where eddies occur.

Buddy line
For added security in stronger currents or limited visibility, buddy pairs should be linked together via a buddy line, which in turn hooks into the main line leading to an SMB.

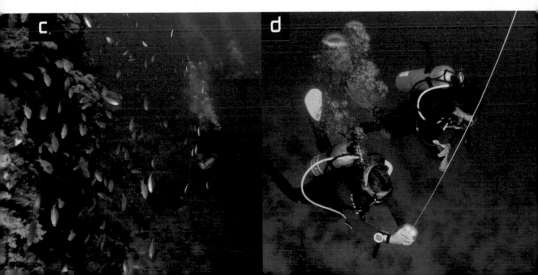

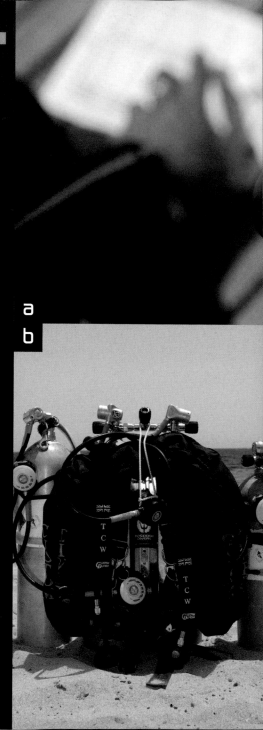

a
b

deep diving

A deep dive is classified by most training organizations as a dive beyond 60 ft (18 m), although perhaps a more realistic estimate is 100 ft (30 m) and deeper.

Deep diving holds a certain mystique, particularly for the novice diver. As a diver becomes more experienced, this feeling often passes, as the most interesting marine life, and the most diverse reefs, are to be found in relatively shallow water. Deep diving is only needed when your objective lies in deep water, such as a wreck or an elusive species of animal. Pushing into deeper water for its own sake often results in an unexciting (and rather short) dive.

Diving at depth

All divers take a genuine risk when they venture beyond 165 ft (50 m) breathing compressed air. The nitrogen content in compressed air becomes narcotic at depth, which can lead to nitrogen narcosis. The condition, named "the rapture of the deep" by Jacques Cousteau, causes a diver to make confused, potentially fatal decisions. Nitrogen also builds up more rapidly in the bloodstream, leading to decompression sickness, and at extreme depths, oxygen itself becomes toxic. To dive safely at greater depths, special gas mixtures are used, in which the balance of oxygen and nitrogen is altered, or new gases are introduced.

a Careful planning
At depth, the possibility of diver error increases due to narcosis, and a clear passage to the surface may not be possible due to decompression demands. Deep dives, therefore, must be carefully planned in advance, and well executed.

b Twin cylinders
An independent alternate air source is essential for any dive below 100 ft (30 m). Many divers who regularly undertake deep dives use twin cylinders, with an independent regulator running off each tank.

c Decompression trapeze
Additional safety items, such as a decompression trapeze (a bar hanging beneath the boat) and an extra cylinder and regulator at the decompression stop, should be available for any dive beyond 165 ft (50 m), demanding lengthy decompression stops.

rescue skills

Most basic dive courses focus on the importance of self-rescue skills, such as the CESA (see pages 92–93). This ensures divers can extract themselves from a hazardous situation, or recognize, and take steps to avoid, a potential emergency.

Rescue training, however, aims to equip divers with the skills to offer assistance to others in the event of an emergency. A combination of first aid and emergency management training, courses range from one-day first aid courses, to advanced medical skills, risk assessment, and team management courses lasting several weeks.

Identifying panic
If you notice your buddy panicking, reassure them with hand signals. Keep your distance, as a flailing arm could knock the regulator from your mouth, or injure you.

Gain attention, and calm
Once you've gained your buddy's attention, and calmed them, ensure that their regulator is in place and they are breathing normally. Take hold of their arm, and initiate a controlled ascent (see pages 90–91).

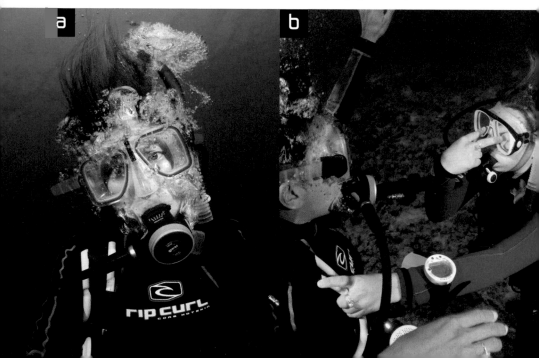

As a safety measure, every diver should undergo basic medical training. First aid courses are rewarding in themselves, and will increase your confidence, making you a safer diver. Your training may also prove invaluable in everyday situations on land, as well as at the dive site.

The key stages for identifying and helping a panicked diver are outlined below, but you should always seek professional training before attempting a rescue.

c Administer oxygen
Once safely out of the water, keep the casualty warm and still. Administer first aid if necessary, and oxygen if decompression sickness is suspected.

d Monitor carefully
Carefully monitor the diver's condition. If it worsens, seek urgent medical help. The casualty may need to be treated in a recompression chamber.

c

d

WATCH IT
see DVD chapter 4

search and salvage

Search and salvage techniques involve working to a prescribed plan to locate and retrieve an item underwater. The search techniques described here can be carried out by recreational divers with a basic level of experience. However, submerged items should only be salvaged by experienced divers. Large items that require the use of lift bags or air lifts (compressed-air equipment for sucking up sand and substrate) should only be retrieved by qualified specialists.

a Rope search

One diver stays at a central point, holding a coiled rope, while a second diver holds the end of the rope and swims in ever-increasing circles, scanning the area. A length of rope is let out each time a set point is reached.

b Grid-pattern search

Two divers follow a set route, with one navigating using a compass while the other searches. The search pattern involves a set number of fin kicks on one heading, a turn of 90°, and a set number on a new heading.

c Marking and recovery

Once located, the item can be marked by securing a line and sending a buoy to the surface. Recovery should only be conducted by experienced divers, and involves using a lift bag, or attaching a line that is hauled up by the support boat.

go dive

coming up...

Planning your dive: 118–125
Thoroughly researching and planning your dive is essential for ensuring a safe, successful experience. Find out more in this chapter.

Diving experiences: 126–133
From exploring freshwater lakes and rivers, to braving the ice-covered waters of the Arctic, there's more to diving than you might expect.

Diving practicalities: 134–139
There are many ways to reach your dive site, whether it's just off the beach or hours away by boat. With live-aboard diving, for example, the site is never more than a few yards away.

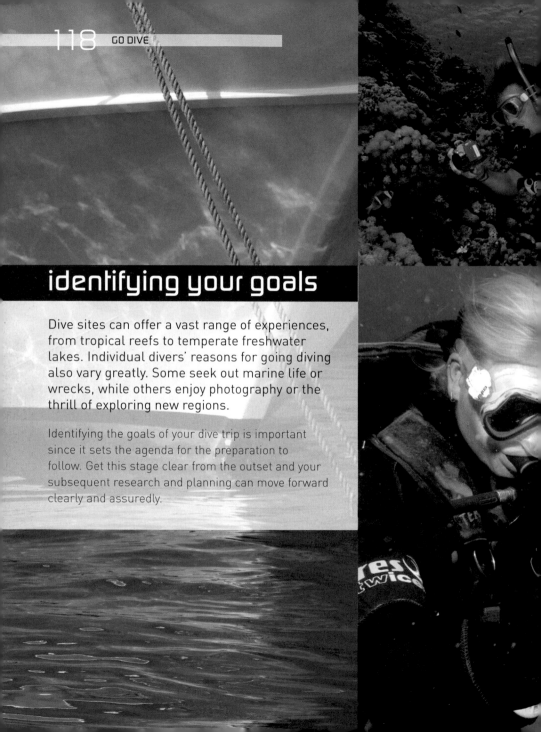

identifying your goals

Dive sites can offer a vast range of experiences, from tropical reefs to temperate freshwater lakes. Individual divers' reasons for going diving also vary greatly. Some seek out marine life or wrecks, while others enjoy photography or the thrill of exploring new regions.

Identifying the goals of your dive trip is important since it sets the agenda for the preparation to follow. Get this stage clear from the outset and your subsequent research and planning can move forward clearly and assuredly.

Factors to consider

There are a number of factors to consider before you can start to plan your dive in more detail:

• Experience and qualifications: a dive should be planned around the least qualified member of the group. Safety is the most important issue, but simple enjoyment is also key, since no one enjoys diving beyond their limits.

• Group specializations: a dive should reflect the broad interests of the divers in the group. Photographers, for example, will require good visibility and interesting features, such as a wreck or a colorful reef.

• Form of diving: the sport takes many forms, such as drift, night, and cave diving, which may require specialized equipment and extra surface support.

finding information

Once you've identified the goals of your dive, you need to decide on a suitable location and operator. Time spent researching in advance is invaluable—particularly for sites you've never dived before—and there's hardly a dive site in the world without a presence on the internet.

The very act of acquiring information can enhance your diving experience. You may learn about the presence of interesting marine life, or discover new areas that you hadn't previously considered. Research will also highlight any potential hazards, allowing you to plan any necessary safety measures.

Where to find information

There are several ways to go about researching a dive site:

- Surf the internet: most dive operators have a website listing their local sites. If you have a particular location in mind, tap it into a search engine. You'll invariably uncover a variety of descriptions, but be wary of biased write-ups.

- Read diving magazines: a good diving magazine will have in-depth articles about specific sites. Many magazines have a dedicated website, too, where you can run a search on your desired site or location.

- Buy a diving guidebook: all of the world's major dive regions have several dedicated guidebooks. In addition to providing diving-specific information, they list local hotels and restaurants, and give details about tourist attractions in the area.

using local knowledge

Dive guides and the internet allow you to make informed decisions, but once you arrive at your destination, local people have the additional information necessary for a safe and truly enjoyable experience.

Careful research and planning is essential for any diving trip, especially if you're organizing an expedition independently. You can obtain information from official bodies, such as the coastguard or harbor authority. They will be aware of shipping activity or commercial work in the area, and should be contacted out of courtesy. Local dive shops are an invaluable source of information, too, but always be aware that you are seeking advice about their local "patch."

Inside information
There's no substitute for local knowledge, and most coastal communities are familiar with the activities of divers. Local people may know the best dive sites and offer advice about nearby land-based attractions. Try dive shops and clubs, boat skippers, fishermen, and residents who know the waters well.

Once you've conducted your research, you must review the conditions at the dive site just prior to your dive. Reference materials grow old, maps and charts may be out of date, and information gleaned from the internet may be inaccurate. For boat dives, make time to talk to the skipper, and visually inspect the conditions at the site if you're diving from the shore.

Having reviewed the site, you can now make preparations for the final briefing. This must cover all aspects of the dive and include not only the divers themselves but everyone else associated with the dive, such as dive marshals and deck hands.

on-site planning

Predive briefing

The briefing should be held as closely as possible to the start of the dive and cover the following points:

- Maximum depth and time limits: these are the key constraining factors.

- Buddy pairs: determine which divers will form buddy pairs—ideally those with similar interests.

- The route: agree on a route for the dive and identify any physical features, or prepare compass headings.

- Safety factors: clarify the safety aspects of the dive, such as the location of communications, first-aid, and oxygen equipment.

Safety considerations

During the site inspection, you should check that the proposed entry and exit points are safe. If you are diving from the shore, you may want to review an alternative exit point, in case conditions deteriorate during the dive.

At the predive briefing, determine a procedure in the event that you, or other divers in the group, become separated, or lost. This is also the time to decide on a way for the dive marshal to recall divers in the event of an incident, such as by banging on the metal ladder at the stern of the boat. Finally, make sure that local emergency contact details are readily available.

diving off a reef

Diving off a tropical coral or temperate rocky reef forms the vast majority of diving experiences for divers throughout the world. There is a staggering array of marine life to be found on a reef, offering the chance of thrilling encounters.

Although these ecosystems give the impression of being robust, and bustling with life, they are in fact extremely delicate. You must adopt a responsible approach when exploring a reef.

WATCH IT
see DVD chapter 5

Golden rules of reef diving

There are certain rules you should follow when diving off a reef:

• Don't touch the reef: if you have no choice (to balance, for example), find a dead or bare patch and use a single finger.

• Don't shine your flashlight into cracks or crevices: any occupants are there for a reason, and being dazzled by a flashlight is extremely distressing for marine life.

• Do pause in one spot: although larger, more charismatic creatures have great appeal, make time to study the smaller reef creatures.

A fragile ecosystem

Coral reefs are particularly vulnerable to being touched or scraped. A coral reef consists of a profusion of tiny creatures called polyps, which are coated in a protective layer. Removing this layer through physical contact exposes the polyp to infection and the risk of disease or death. Rocky reefs are also vulnerable: an area of seemingly bare rock may be colonized by microscopic organisms, which can be destroyed or displaced at the slightest touch.

wreck diving

The ghostly image of a wreck is one of the most evocative in diving, combining mystery, adventure, and large gatherings of marine life. Behind every wreck is a story of heroism, incompetence, skullduggery, or tragedy—an irresistible draw for divers with a thirst for exploration.

Viewed through human eyes, wrecks are clearly man-made, but for marine life they offer flat surfaces to colonize, and nooks and crannies to use as hiding places or ambush points. As smaller fish are drawn to wrecks to feed on algae or crusting organisms, so larger predators follow, and the profusion of life around a wreck can be extraordinary.

WATCH IT
see DVD chapter 5

Safety considerations

Wrecks are safe when dived from the outside, simply representing an angular reef. Only when penetrated can they become dangerous: the interior of a wreck can be confusing, with poor visibility and twisting passageways. Consider the following when planning your dive:

• Penetrating a wreck is mostly unnecessary. You can safely explore it from the exterior to appreciate the bustling marine life.

• You should prepare for a wreck penetration in the same way as you would for cave diving (see pages 132–133). Laying guidelines is essential, as is an independent alternate air source, at least two flashlights, and a clear plan of exploration. Additional training and relevant qualifications are also necessary.

freshwater sites

Most diving around the world takes place in the sea, but freshwater ecosystems also have much to offer the diver.

Rivers provide great opportunities for drift diving, and fish are often tolerant and inquisitive as they rarely come into contact with divers. Look out for gatherings of fish in deep pools, or on bends. Lakes provide a more traditional, but often excellent diving experience. For example, Lake Malawi in Africa (below) has more fish species than Europe and North America combined.

What you need to consider

Always consider the following points before you dive in freshwater:

- Other water users: be especially wary of boaters, anglers, and other recreational water users, as activity is likely to be heavier than in the sea.

- Ownership: many freshwater systems, particularly rivers, are privately owned and you require special permission before diving.

- Altitude: you may need to use special dive tables for lakes and rivers situated above sea level.

Freshwater diving skills

Diving in freshwater systems requires a specialized set of diving skills:

- Good buoyancy control: you will be less buoyant in freshwater than in saltwater, so you must be able to refine your buoyancy control.

- Controlled fin kicks: lake beds often consist of fine substrate and demand controlled fin kicks— as well as excellent buoyancy control—to keep from disturbing the bottom.

ice diving and cave diving

Ice diving and cave diving are both classed as overhead environment diving, meaning that there is no direct ascent to the surface. Diving in these conditions is a specialized skill, and should not be undertaken lightly. Experience, appropriate training, and good logistical support are all essential for a safe dive.

Double hood
You will need two thick hoods to protect your head from the cold.

Cold-water regulator
A specially modified regulator is less susceptible to the extreme cold.

Dry-glove system
A dry glove system will keep your hands warm and functioning.

Ice diving

Conducted in an eerie environment where light and sound are muted, ice diving involves exploring lake or ocean systems, either through a hole in the ice, or by diving beneath glaciers. Specialized equipment is needed, as conventional gear is not reliable at extreme temperatures. Thermal protection is essential.

Cave diving
A truly elite sport, cave diving is one of the most extreme forms of diving. A diver many miles into a cave system is as isolated as an astronaut should a problem occur, and must be self-reliant. Cave diving calls for the use of navigational guidelines, complex gas mixtures, scooters, specialized light systems, and a level of commitment and cool-headedness seldom found in any other area of extreme sports.

diving from a boat

Most dive sites are only accessible by boat, making boat diving by far the most common way to dive. However, just as dive sites themselves vary, so do the types of boat available. Boats range from tiny kayaks to huge vessels that can cross oceans.

Boat diving has clear advantages: sites not accessible from shore can be explored with ease, the boat can act as a self-contained diving and accommodation unit, drifting divers can be tracked, and it's easy to deploy and recover divers. Most dive operators have their own vessels, although dive boats can be chartered independently.

Dive boat essentials

Although diving can be conducted from almost any vessel, a dive boat should be equipped with the proper safety equipment, and certain procedures should be followed:

- Communication and safety equipment, such as flares, signaling devices, and a first-aid kit, must be present.

- There must be enough oxygen on board to treat a casualty until a decompression chamber can be reached.

- Life rafts should be large enough to accommodate everyone on board, and be well maintained.

- There should be a simple means of deploying and recovering divers, such as a diving platform.

- Divers should receive a comprehensive boat briefing from the skipper, including full safety information.

diving from the shore

Coastal diving involves accessing the dive site from the shore, and is many divers' introduction to the sport. Diving just off the coast means the site is readily accessible, and divers can conduct an entire trip simply and inexpensively as a buddy pair, without the need for boat support.

The coastal margins are also where the vast majority of marine life congregates, which is a strong attraction for most divers. Shallow water, and the presence of a firm substrate within reach of the Sun's rays, creates busy reefs, which in turn draw larger species from the open ocean.

Coastal diving essentials

There are certain safety issues, specific to coastal diving, that you need to take into consideration when planning your dive:

- Be aware of the movement of tides and currents in the area. Certain sites may only be accessible during low tide.

- Pay extra attention to boat traffic, which may be heavy on popular stretches of coastline, particularly off beaches.

- When planning your entry and exit points, it's a good idea to have an alternative exit point as a backup, in case your first choice is unusable.

- Visibility may be poor near the shore due to suspended particles in the water column and wave action. Be wary of pollution near the coast.

diving from a live-aboard

Live-aboard dive vessels offer a self-contained diving experience where the entry point to the dive site is never more than a ship's length away. The modern live-aboard is essentially a small cruise liner, forming a hotel, a dive center, and a safety support vessel in one.

Live-aboard diving is one of the most intense diving experiences for the recreational diver, offering long-range trips and nonstop diving throughout the voyage. Many live-aboard vessels offer mixed-gas diving and rebreather equipment, and most have facilities for photography and filming.

Live-aboard diving essentials

Carefully inspect a dive operator before signing up for a live-aboard expedition. Live-aboards demand a superior level of self-sufficiency, and should be fully equipped:

- Extensive medical equipment, and suitably qualified personnel, are a prerequisite.

- Excellent communication facilities are vital. Live-aboards, by their very nature, venture beyond the reach of shore-based operators, and are often the only way to dive isolated reefs and wrecks, or encounter marine wildlife in the open ocean.

- State-of-the-art safety equipment should be carried, appropriate to the size of the boat, and the number of people on board.

- The modern live-aboard is essentially a small cruise liner, and should offer a similar standard of care and service.

go further

coming up...

Technical diving: 144–147

Technical diving really takes the sport to the next level. By using a mixture of gases, divers can explore at greater depths and for longer periods of time. Rebreather diving, where exhaled breath is recycled rather than expelled, is also becoming increasingly popular.

Diving specializations: 148–151

Turning diving into a career holds great appeal for many recreational divers. The reality of professional diving can mean a demanding workplace, but for those with the dedication to succeed, the lifestyle rewards can be enormous.

technical diving—mixed gas

Technical divers seek to extend their range within the water, whether by going deeper than is possible using normal air, or by staying underwater for longer periods of time. Technical diving using gas mixtures is growing in popularity, and is no longer seen as the exclusive preserve of an elite few.

Technical divers frequently operate beyond the range of rescue, or in environments where there is no clear path to the surface. The margin for error is extremely slim, and such divers continue to push the boundaries of technology and exploration.

Gear configuration— front view

Colored regulators
The regulator second stages are individually colored to indicate specific gas mixtures.

Wing-style BCD
A wing-style BCD has increased lift ability for twin cylinders and bulky equipment.

Gas mixtures

Technical diving involves the use of gas mixtures that decrease the decompression penalties of breathing normal air. This may be either through increasing the percentage of oxygen in the mix (nitrox diving), or by introducing additional gases such as helium (trimix diving). Nitrox diving is the most common—and least extreme—form of technical diving. Trimix diving requires specialized training and equipment, including the use of computer programs designed to plan and simulate dives using a variety of gas mixtures.

Gear configuration— back view

Extra cylinders
Additional air cylinders containing special gas mixes are carried in the front.

Manifold
An isolation manifold connects twin cylinders, and a central valve allows each to be used independently.

WATCH IT
see DVD chapter 6

technical diving—rebreathers

Rebreather diving is at the cutting edge of the sport, and involves the use of a closed breathing loop that recycles the diver's exhaled breath.

Chemicals remove carbon dioxide from the exhaled air, while enough oxygen is introduced into the system to sustain life. Rebreather diving allows for greatly decreased air consumption, and no exhaust bubbles to alarm sgeartish marine life. The need for specialized training and careful gear preparation, however, means it remains a specialized area.

Closed-circuit rebreather equipment

The closed-circuit rebreather (CCR) recycles a diver's breath, only dumping gas during the ascent. A chemical in the scrubbing unit absorbs carbon dioxide from the exhaled gas, and a mixture of pure oxygen and air is introduced into the loop to maintain a safe, breathable mixture.

Path of oxygen from cylinder to scrubbing unit

Exhaled air flows into scrubbing unit

Oxygen flows into scrubbing unit

Breathable air flows from scrubbing unit to mouthpiece

Intake hose
Cleaned, breathable air flows from the scrubbing unit and back to the diver's mouthpiece

Exhaust hose
Exhaled air flows from the mouthpiece, and into the scrubbing unit, via this hose.

Oxygen cylinder
Pure oxygen held in this tank is added to the breathing loop, replacing that used by the diver.

Scrubbing unit
An absorbant chemical in the scrubbing unit removes CO_2 from the diver's exhaled breath.

Air cylinder
The air held in this tank is introduced into the system to maintain the overall volume of gas.

Data display
The diver can check the rebreather's gas content, and monitor toxicity, on a computer display.

WATCH IT
see DVD chapter 6

photography and videography

Divers have long had a strong urge to photograph and film the extraordinary creatures found beneath the waves.

Once the preserve of a select few, underwater photography and videography has exploded in popularity thanks to digital technology. With ever smaller cameras and underwater housings, capturing underwater images has never been easier.

Underwater equipment

Digital cameras may provide instant feedback (perhaps the one thing photographers yearned for during the years of slides and film), but not necessarily instant success. Light behaves very differently underwater, and there is a real art to taking good pictures. The first step is to use the correct underwater gear.

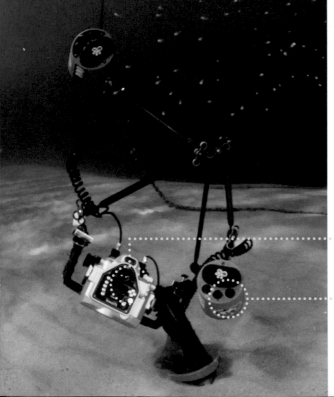

Waterproof housing
A large housing protects your camera, and offers excellent access to the controls.

Light source or "strobe"
Strobes on flexible arms distance the light sources from the lens, and allow the subject to be lit from different angles.

WATCH IT
see DVD chapter 6

Camera techniques

Follow these key techniques, as used by professional underwater photographers and filmmakers, to help you improve the quality of your own stills and films:

- Familiarize yourself with the camera on land—the controls will be harder to use underwater.

- Keep the light source away from the lens to prevent backscatter (light reflecting off particles in the water).

- Get close to your subject to fill the frame, make the shot clearer, and reduce backscatter.

- Shoot upward, so the subject isn't lost against a reef, or the seabed.

- With video, shoot to a preconceived plan. There is nothing worse than a 40-minute video from a 40-minute dive!

conservation and expedition diving

Most divers enter the sport because of an interest in marine life, and an urge to experience adventure and excitement. For this reason, conservation and expedition diving projects are becoming increasingly popular. More and more divers are eager to seek out unique or remote sites around the world, and help preserve marine ecosystems under threat from human activities.

Conservation diving

A number of organizations run programs where volunteer divers can gather scientific data, or help in the creation of nature reserves. Volunteers generally receive basic scientific training and work under the supervision of qualified staff, who will monitor the data. Such programs can be highly effective: the establishment of the Belize Barrier Reef as a World Heritage Site was largely due to the efforts of volunteers. It is, however, always worth investigating an organization claiming to run scientific or conservation programs. A quick internet search will reveal the extent of their work, and the validity of their claims.

Expedition diving

Through live-aboard diving vessels, and resorts in remote locations, most dive sites around the world are accessible to the recreational diver. There do remain, however, a number of little-known sites where a well-planned expedition is required to gain access. Such sites offer excitement and new experiences, but, being remote, present inherent dangers. Severe accidents can be magnified if the casualty is far from medical aid— treatment will be necessary on-site, with evacuation required for further medical care. All diving expeditions, whether organized by a dive operator or independently by a group of qualified divers, should be meticulously planned, using highly experienced leaders or diving professionals.

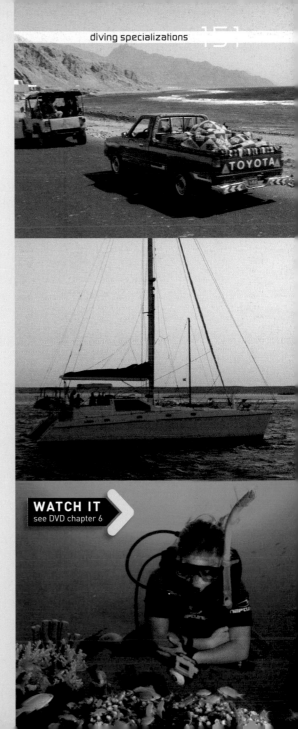

WATCH IT
see DVD chapter 6

diving on the web

Listed below is a small selection of diving websites from around the world, containing everything from training organizations, dive operators, and conservation organizations, to online magazines and regional information.

US and CANADA resources

www.padi.com
An extremely useful site from the Professional Association of Diving Instructors, the largest training organization in the world. In addition to providing course information, the site lists approved dive operators throughout the world.

www.diversalertnetwork.org
Provides an international network of diver medics, and decompression chambers. The Divers Alert Network also arranges insurance packages for traveling divers.

www.dtmag.com
This site, from the producers of Dive Training magazine, provides a useful listing of dive sites and operators throughout the US.

www.divermag.com
Canada's long-running Diver magazine has an online presence with lots of information about dive sites and operators.

www.conservefish.org/site
The Marine Fish Conservation Network is dedicated to conserving marine fish and promoting their long-term sustainability.

www.hds.org
This is the online home of the Historical Diving Society USA, which investigates and keeps accurate records of diving history.

UK and IRELAND resources

www.bsac.com
The British Sub Aqua Club is the original British diving training organization, and runs courses aimed specifically at divers learning in the temperate waters around the UK.

www.irishunderwatercouncil.com
The Irish Underwater Council is Ireland's national diving organization. It offers internationally recognized qualifications, and has over 70 affiliated clubs across the country.

AUSTRALIA and NEW ZEALAND resources

www.divenewzealand.com
The online version of Dive New Zealand magazine provides information about operators, marine life, and dive sites in New Zealand.

www.underwater.com.au
Underwater offers information about diving in Australia, as well as in the Indo-Pacific, which many consider to be the best of all dive regions.

SOUTH AFRICA resources

www.divesouthafrica.com
Provides general information about diving in South Africa, and includes details for Mozambique.

dive talk

A-clamp fitting—a type of fitting for attaching a regulator first stage to a pillar valve.

Alternate air source (AAS)—a reserve air supply, such as an octopus second stage or a pony cylinder.

Ambient pressure—the total pressure acting on a body at a given depth.

Ascent—to return from depth to the surface at the end of a dive.

Atmospheric pressure—the pressure exerted by the gases in the atmosphere, equal to 1 BAR (14.7 PSI) at sea level.

Boyle's law—a physical law stating that the volume of a gas is inversely proportional to the pressure exerted on it.

Bubble check—an underwater inspection of another diver's equipment to determine if it has any major air leaks.

Buddy—a diver who assists their assigned diving partner before, during, and after a dive.

Buddy line—a safety line for tethering a buddy pair together.

Buoyancy compensation device (BCD)—a jacket that can be inflated and deflated, allowing a diver to control their buoyancy.

Buoyancy control—to manipulate buoyancy by using the BCD and controlled breathing.

Decompression—to return to the conditions of normal atmospheric pressure by controlled means, such as decompression stops.

Decompression sickness (DCS)—a potentially serious medical condition resulting from the formation of nitrogen bubbles in the bloodstream and tissues of the body.

Decompression stop—a scheduled pause in a diver's ascent to allow nitrogen to pass from the body's tissues back into the blood at a safe rate.

Depth gauge—a gauge that measures ambient pressure, and uses it to give a depth reading.

Descent—to travel from the surface to depth.

DIN fitting—a screw-thread fitting for attaching a regulator first stage to a pillar valve.

Dive computer—a digital device that provides a diver with information such as depth, dive time, and rate of ascent.

D-ring—a D-shaped ring found on the BCD, used for attaching equipment.

Drysuit—an exposure suit designed for use in very cold waters.

Equalization—to equalize the pressure between the inner and outer ear by performing the Valsalva maneuver.

Exposure suit—a suit, such as a wetsuit, worn to prevent excessive loss of body heat in the water.

Finning—kicking the feet rhythmically while wearing fins to move through the water.

First stage—a component of the regulator that reduces high pressure air from the cylinder and allows it to pass to the second stage for inhalation by a diver.

Mask squeeze—discomfort caused by increasing water pressure acting on a diver's mask and pressing it into the face.

Neoprene—a synthetic rubber fabric with good heat insulation properties used to make exposure suits.

Nitrogen narcosis—intoxication caused by breathing nitrogen at depth.

Nitrox—a breathable gas mixture containing nitrogen and oxygen, usually with a greater content of oxygen than found in air.

Octopus second stage—a reserve second stage, carried by divers in the event of the main second stage failing, or for use by their buddy.

O-ring—a ring-shaped gasket, used to seal interfaces between pressurized pieces of equipment, such as in the pillar valve.

Overhead environment—any diving environment where direct access to the surface is restricted, such as inside a cave or under ice.

Pillar valve—the valve that transfers gas from the cylinder to the regulator first stage.

Pony cylinder—a small cylinder of breathable gas with an independent regulator, intended for emergency use.

Rebreather—a breathing apparatus that recycles a diver's exhaled air.

Recompression chamber—a pressure chamber used in the treatment of divers suffering from decompression sickness.

RIB (rigid inflatable boat)—a fast utility boat with a V-shaped hull and an inflatable tube running around its upper edge.

Safety stop—a precautionary pause in a diver's ascent (usually for three minutes at about 20 ft (6 m) below the surface) to prevent the formation of nitrogen bubbles in the bloodstream.

SCUBA—acronym for Self-Contained Underwater Breathing Apparatus.

Second stage—a component of the regulator that delivers air at a breathable pressure as and when a diver inhales.

SPG (submersible pressure gauge)—an instrument that displays the remaining quantity of gas in a diver's cylinder.

Test date—the date when a compressed gas cylinder was last hydrostatically tested.

Trim—the posture and balance of a diver underwater.

Valsalva maneuver—exhaling while keeping the lips closed and pinching the nose to force air into the middle ear to equalize pressure.

Water column—the zone of water between the surface and the seabed.

Weight belt—a belt, worn around the waist, that is designed to carry a diver's lead ballast.

Wetsuit—an exposure suit made of neoprene rubber, which traps a thin layer of water against the skin as an insulating medium.

index

and finally...

Thanks from the author
Monty Halls would like to thank Oceanic dive gear, Suunto, Fourth Element clothing, Gates Housings, and Ocean Reef for their support over the years. Many thanks also to everyone on the Great Ocean Adventures team, particularly Matthew Frank for making it all possible, and Scubazoo for their excellent images, both moving and still. Thanks also to the DK team for being so tolerant of my itinerant lifestyle while getting this book done. Thanks of course—as ever—to Antje for just being Antje.

Thanks from Dorling Kindersley
DK would like to thank Juan Camilo Martinez, Hany Iraky, Michelle-Ann Onn Lin Loh, Mark Rogers, Charlie Todd, and Daniel Uren for modeling, Ed Poore at Poseidon, and Tony Backhurst Scuba. We would also like to thank Tarda Davison-Aitkins for editorial assistance, Katie Eke for design assistance, and Margaret McCormack for indexing.

Thanks for the pictures
The publisher would like to thank the following for their kind permission to reproduce their photographs: **Alamy Images**: Chris A. Crumley 116; Reinhard Dirscherl 109bl; David Fleetham 12–13; Images of Africa Photobank 130bl; Jeff Rotman 14–15. **Dan Burton**:132bl. **Corbis**: Ralph A. Clevenger 27t; Brandon D. Cole 131br; Stephen Frink 128br; Gray Hardel 26b; Rick Price 132tr; Reuters 25; Jeffrey L. Rotman 129bl, 133bl; Henry Watkins & Yibran Aragon/Reuters 133t. **DK Images**: Rough Guides 50b. **Getty Images**: The Image Bank/Michael Melford 27b. All other images © Dorling Kindersley. For further information see: **www.dkimages.com**

But be careful...
Scuba diving is potentially hazardous—all participants must assume responsibility for their own actions and safety. Neither the author nor the publisher can be held responsible for any accidents resulting from following any of the activities shown in this book. Always prepare for the unexpected and be cautious.

About the author
Marine biologist and former Royal Marines officer, Monty Halls has been diving since 1984. He has led expeditions all over the world, including a multinational team in southeast India that located the ruins of a lost civilization. Monty co-wrote Eyewitness Companions: Scuba Diving for Dorling Kindersley, and has presented television programs for Sky TV, Channel 4, and National Geographic Channel, as well as Channel 5/Discovery Europe's Great Ocean Adventures.